London Borough of Tower Hamlets

910000008056300

KT-436-314

Teeñage ⌣
Depression

WITHDRAWN

First symptoms of depression often occur during teenage years, and it can be a disturbing and confusing time for families as well as the teenager themselves. How can you tell whether it is just typical teenage ups and downs that will pass, or something more serious? How can we reliably identify and support teenagers with depression?

In this book experienced clinician and researcher Gordon Parker explains how to systematically identify different mood disorders and contributing factors. He and co-author Kerrie Eyers explain when clinical treatment is required and outline treatment options. They also discuss the particular challenges faced by adolescents and approaches to effective management.

Drawing on insightful personal accounts from teenagers and young adults about their experiences, and based on extensive clinical research, this is essential reading for every parent, carer or professional looking after a young person with depression.

Gordon Parker is Scientia Professor of Psychiatry at the University of New South Wales and Executive Director of the Black Dog Institute, Sydney, Australia. He is a renowned researcher with over 30 years' experience with mood disorders, and is author of *Dealing with Depression: A common sense guide to mood disorders.*

Kerrie Eyers is a psychologist, teacher and editor with many years' experience in mental health, based at the Black Dog Institute, Sydney, Australia.

GORDON PARKER & KERRIE EYERS

NAVIGATING TEENAGE DEPRESSION

A guide for parents and professionals

Routledge
Taylor & Francis Group

LONDON AND NEW YORK

First published in Australia in 2009
By Allen & Unwin Pty Ltd

First published in the UK in 2010
by Routledge
27 Church Road, Hove, East Sussex BN3 2FA

Simultaneously published in the USA and Canada
by Routledge
711 Third Avenue, New York NY 10017

Routledge is an imprint of the Taylor & Francis Group, an informa business

Copyright © Black Dog Institute 2009

Cover illustration by Andrew Joyner/Matthew Johnstone
Cover design by Lisa White

All rights reserved. No part of this book may be reprinted or reproduced or
utilised in any form or by any electronic, mechanical, or other means, now
known or hereafter invented, including photocopying and recording, or in any
information storage or retrieval system, without permission in writing from the
publishers.

British Library Cataloguing in Publication Data
A catalogue record for this book is available from the British Library

Library of Congress Cataloging in Publication Data
Parker, Gordon, 1942–
  Navigating teenage depression: a guide for parents and professionals/Gordon
Parker & Kerrie Eyers.
     p. cm.
  Includes bibliographical references and index.
  ISBN 978-0-415-58337-4 (pbk.)
  1. Depression in adolescence. I. Eyers, Kerrie. II. Title.
  RJ506.D4P37 2010
  616.85'2700835—dc22   2010001479

ISBN: 978-0-415-58337-4 (pbk only)

To John Bevins

This book is dedicated to John Bevins. John has been a friend to the Black Dog Institute from its beginnings—in conceiving the evocative logo and providing, through his advertising agency, the covers of its yearly reports, salient banners and much else besides. He has also assisted us, in particular, to identify what the Institute's constituency expects of us. We have learnt from John that 'it all comes down to empathy', and we hope this book respects this principle.

Contents

Preface

Adolescence is a period of rapid changes. Between the ages of twelve and seventeen, for example, a parent ages as much as twenty years. **Author unknown**

A teenager at their best is a powerhouse and a joy to have around; their mastery of the often too accurate put-down, delivered gently or with searing scorn, keeps us on our toes.

But when they themselves are 'put down' by a mood disorder such as depression, life changes—for them and those around them. Those who care for them, in all senses of the word—be they parents, teachers, relatives, friends—may find the intensity of a teenager's distress blinding. Of equal concern is when depression causes the young person to retreat from the world and deny that there are any problems. In this case, they might mask their anguish by becoming 'invisible', withdrawing until, like the Cheshire Cat in *Alice in Wonderland*, only the memory of their smile remains.

Should you approach a teenager who seems to be having difficulties, or should you 'leave well enough alone'? Or *is* the situation 'well enough'? Can you wait it out—whatever 'it' is? What is the logic for helping when depression can be so variable in severity, so changeable in its manifestations—and, at times, can put the young person at risk of suicide or self-injury? What *is* the best way to go forward?

After many years as a clinician, I formally detail here a model that I have found useful for dealing with mood disorders, and invite you into the world of clinical assessment. This book presents some of the reasoning that takes place on my side of the desk.

My viewpoint has been developed over many years of research, and the model is followed in clinical assessments undertaken at the Black Dog Institute, a Sydney-based clinical research facility with educational and community programs seeking to advance understanding of the mood disorders. Such reasoning, however, does not need to remain solely within the province of the clinician. As parents or carers, your observations, judgments and day-to-day encouragement form the keystone in the clinical arch that supports a young person in distress, and which can assist clinical decisions.

My ambition over the years has been to champion the assertion that depression is not an 'it'—not a 'one-size-fits-all' disorder. This is not, regrettably, the current model for charting mood disorders, which more commonly posits 'depression' as a single condition, merely varying by severity.

The Black Dog Institute's clinical approach is derived from this assertion: that there are differing mood disorders, with differing causes, and requiring quite differing management strategies. That the Institute's model is in the minority makes it neither 'right' nor 'wrong'. It is, however, in comparison to many other ways of viewing depression, able to be articulated. Thus, you can judge for yourself.

The information presented in this book will, we hope, make you better armed and more assured of what you are doing, sharpen your observations and expectations, and assist you with key decisions. Our approach argues against chance and guesswork—which are often the only options available to most parents and carers. It offers a logic for assessing a young person's moods, the causes of such moods, and their best management—and, most importantly, whether there is a 'disorder' at all.

In 2007 and 2008, we published books that reported ways of gaining control over depression and bipolar disorder, based on stories from hundreds of individuals recounting their path to diagnosis and how they had subsequently kept the 'black dog' at bay.[1] We adopt a similar model in this book, selecting material from the 'other' experts: the teenagers who have recovered from their mood disorder, or brought it under control. These teenagers generously contributed to the Black Dog Institute essay competition topic, 'Mood Disorders in Adolescence—Grassroots Solutions'. In the essay extracts that appear in this book, each contributor has been given a pseudonym to protect their privacy.

We have also been blessed with detailed feedback from three generous parents who have lived through mood swings in their teenager: yet another perspective. All views ('outside in' views from clinicians and parents, and 'inside out' perspectives from our teenage essayists) add to the 'democracy of knowledge'.

Kerrie Eyers and I hope that we can provide you, the reader, with a professional frame of reference: a map for guiding you and your charge through the maze of teenage depression and out the other side.

Gordon Parker
Black Dog Institute
www.blackdoginstitute.org.au

1. Navigating the maze
Three stories of teenage depression

It's as if someone had tied a brick around my heart and was daring me to swim. **Amy**

Consider the following scenario, which comes from an essay called 'My Life as a Movie' written by Leah, an adolescent girl in distress. Imagine that she has come to you—a friend or a relative—because she is depressed and feels that the professional help she has had so far has not assisted. How would you respond to her plight? How would you judge and weigh the many circumstances that are causing her distress? How might she best be helped by a professional?

Leah's story is confronting: she is dealing with a complex set of difficulties. Her circumstances illustrate how teenage depression can be a tangle of many threads—genetic, psychological, physical and situational. By sharing her story and those of others, we hope that this book can help you to map sure pathways through the maze. We have started by jumping in at the deep end, but will provide you with directions as you navigate through the chapters.

I was sixteen when I was diagnosed with depression—although, in hindsight, it started much earlier. I remember crying myself to sleep when I was about nine years old, engulfed in a terrible grief I couldn't comprehend, let alone explain.

It had always been a daily struggle for Mum to get me to go to school, just as it was a daily struggle for me to stay home. For me, school was an exhausting exercise in simply keeping my head above water and flying below the radar. I felt ten years older than my peers and isolated from my teachers. I felt as if I knew terrible truths about the world they would never understand. Mum used to tell me not to worry, that they were just afraid of me because I was smarter than they were. Of course this was meant to cheer me up, but I was struck with a huge sense of aloneness. Is this the way I would feel about other people forever?

Mum spent a lot of time in hospital after her first nervous breakdown. We (my dad, my older sister and younger brother) coped with her bipolar disorder as best we could. I always had the impression that there was only room in our house for one crazy person. And Mum was it. Despite the truth of my own condition playing out in front of me, I still came to believe I was the way I was simply because I was a bad person. A lazy person. A stupid person. I may have felt I was carrying the heavy heart of someone twice my age but in many of the most important ways, I was still just a kid. I decided that if I couldn't be happy, I'd just pretend. It was too hard to deal with Mum's illness, let alone my own. One day I came home from school and she was in bed so I sat down with her. It wasn't until halfway through the conversation that I realised she didn't seem to know what was going on. She didn't even know who I was.

For the past few years, with Mum not around, Dad working hard and my siblings and I at the age where we couldn't stand to be in the same room as each other for more than five minutes without coming to blows, I found comfort where I could. I daydreamed at every opportunity, escaping to made-up places where all I had to do was find treasure and fight evil. It's much easier to be brave when faced with a fire-breathing dragon than faced with your own demons. I lost myself in movies and books and music and drawing, loved nothing more than long stretches of time as someone else. Anyone else. I sought quick fixes in food, and snacking became synonymous with being warm and safe and home.

By the time I was in Year 7, I had almost perfected the art of faking it. With my sunny demeanour and dry humour, I had earned myself plenty of friends. I was, as far as anyone knew, dizzyingly happy. I decided to make a fresh start in high school and was looking forward to feeling better. Losing weight, working harder in class, even talking to boys. This naive vision lasted less than a week and, by the first Friday, I had already been branded 'the fat girl'. Of course, as any teenager will tell you, fat girls are not just fat. Fat girls are automatically also stupid, ugly and absolutely worthless. And so the bullying that began slowly and subtly in primary school has continued and intensified throughout high school.

I haven't ever discussed the bullying with my family. Nor with my teachers. If nothing else, I still have my pride and, to me, admitting to the bullying was worse than coping with the bullying itself. I would not give anyone the satisfaction of knowing they had hurt me. As such, school continued to be the hellish place where I had no rights. No right to feel safe or happy or even be treated like much of a human being at all. Pretty soon, my peers had taught me about how I deserved to be treated and I became my own worst bully.

So I retreated to the place I was always safe and began spending most of my free time at home. I decided to focus my energy on becoming what I considered to be a model child.

I cooked dinner for the family, made myself responsible for my mum's wellbeing, and skipped all the obligatory adolescent pastimes like sneaking out, drinking, and generally rebelling. I became intensely angry at my parents for the smallest criticism, as if betrayed by my only allies. I knew deep down that they wanted nothing more than for me to be healthy and happy and to play up like a normal teenager, but my deepening depression had poisoned every part of my mind. Rage had become my default reaction to anything that threatened to push me to face my aforementioned demons.

The years became a blur, a mess of raw emotion. I can't remember how it happened but in Year 10, when Mum was getting better, they started to see that things were just not right with me. I changed schools twice (I attended four different high schools by the end of Year 12), a friend of mine committed suicide, my grandmother died, my final year exam was disastrous. I had no aspirations, no expectations of the future, no plans. I held on tightly to my last sliver of hope that things could only get easier.

WHAT'S GOING ON?

What do you think are the most important factors in Leah's situation? Do you think she has a serious problem with the way she is feeling, or is it one that you expect will simply pass with time?

If you think Leah's situation is serious, what indicators or flags make you think so—and what do you think are the risks to her condition?

Some reflections from Leah's story

Leah has a longstanding set of problems, starting with low moods since late childhood, school avoidance, and a persistent lack of pleasure in anything. She is old before her time, clever and perceptive. She and her two siblings have had to shoulder some serious early responsibility: their father works hard and their mentally ill mother is remote or absent. Leah's main defences have been daydreaming and, in the company of friends, a mask of dry humour and pretended happiness.

Comfort eating has led to a weight problem for Leah, and more recently the onset of puberty and its cascade of hormonal changes means added self-consciousness as she becomes aware of boys, and her peers start to behave in the way that can be characteristic of this age group, branding her 'the fat girl' and marring her tentative dreams of a fresh start in high school. She has learnt to incorporate their views and now regards herself as 'bad', 'lazy' and 'stupid'. She has become her 'own worst bully'.

Over time she withdraws to home, her last refuge, and becomes the 'model child' in an attempt to control what is happening to her and to elicit care by giving care. Here, however, her self-restriction and the impossibility of perfection threaten to shatter her brittle facade and pitch her into frustration and anger. Four moves in high school, the suicide of a friend, the death of a loved grandmother and poor performance in the final high school exams all add to a powerful mix—one that may also include a genetic leaning to mood dysregulation and depression conferred by her mother. So Leah is dealing with a cascade of genes, temperament, environment and stressors.

As you read her story, you might have had a mix of questions. What is happening for her? How serious is it? And what might you—or *should* you—do about it? Leah is, clearly, struggling.

Leah says she has been diagnosed with 'depression'. If this is correct, is her depression a 'primary' disorder, or is it 'secondary' to some other condition, such as anxiety?

If she is depressed, what is driving her disorder? There are many possibilities here. Her mother has had a 'nervous breakdown' and has been diagnosed with a 'bipolar disorder'. Has Leah, then, developed a genetically underpinned mood disorder, initially presenting with 'smouldering' indefinite symptoms (e.g. crying herself to sleep, loneliness, school resistance)? Is her 'condition' still evolving, or is it now established, allowing a clear diagnosis?

Or are Leah's symptoms secondary—a response to living with a troubled mother she regards as 'crazy', and to her other home circumstances?

Perhaps her distress stems from her own self-disparaging views (seeing herself as bad, lazy and stupid)—and if so, how did she develop those self-judgments? Are such self-judgments personality-based or are they 'introjections' of the voices of others who might have described her in such unsympathetic and judgmental ways?

How much of Leah's deep unhappiness emerges from other family factors—including her father being distanced by his work, and tension with her siblings? Has her diet ('quick fixes' and 'snacking') actually compounded her misery—either as an unsuccessful self-consolatory strategy, or by directly compromising her health? And has it contributed to her being overweight and then being demeaned at school as the 'fat girl' and subsequently bullied? Or, as Leah implies, has the prolonged bullying across primary and secondary school been central to her distress—making her judge school as 'hellish' and so perturbing that she could not discuss it with anyone?

And how to factor in the social issues that then came into play—the changes of schools, the loss of a friend to suicide, her poor final examination results and her lack of career plans? Are they secondary factors that might disappear if the primary problem was addressed? Are they additional development-related factors—or consequences of her depression?

You can generate a wide range of possible explanations, with each prioritising some factors above others—and more importantly, each leading to quite differing ways of providing help. The risks are many. It is tempting to rush in and seize on some single explanatory factor to provide reassurance—and, sometimes, to silence further discussion. It is human nature to seek to resolve ambiguity by imposing an all-explanatory cause—as much to settle our own disquiet as to try to assist people in distress. Which makes it all too easy to then suggest they seek help from a professional from the 'wrong' discipline—be it a counsellor, general practitioner (GP), psychologist, school counsellor, hypnotherapist or whoever.

Let's consider a second scenario. This piece, called 'The Death Notices', was posted by sixteen-year-old Kath onto her Facebook site. Imagine that you have known Kath over the years—that you are a family friend, or a relative—and that Kath has never struck you as having any particular ongoing problems. And now you are referred to a copy of this posting by your daughter.

I was good at being sad.

My best friend was good at handwriting. Hers was beautiful. My other best friend could play piano, she could play anything. My worst enemy did pretty. She did 'pretty' REALLY well. At local high school make-up was hunted down with a vengeance by the teachers, but Worst Enemy didn't need it. Her adorable looks won gold long before the rest of us got within a *Dolly*'s cover pix of that amber bronze blush compact.

I was the expert on sad.

Sad started about Thursday, built its crescendo by Friday and peaked on Saturday. Sunday was for getting through, but with Monday coming, by then I was on my way up.

If I wasn't sufficiently sad by Friday night I would pick up the newspaper and read, reread and re-reread every, single, one, of, the, death notices. While my own mum was busy cooking dinner I sobbed for these unknown lost beloveds. I cried over the babies, mothers, wives, teenagers and Nanna Sadly Missed In Our Hearts Forever with the little black rose motif.

My Dearest Daddy I Miss You So Now You Are With The Angels didn't ever do much for me so I hurried through those to the peacefully sleeping/lost/departed/really dead Mums, Nannas, Beloved Daughters and Sons. Yes, well, that's enough said on that and my reasons for sad.

I had been reading death notices and crying since I was ten, so I knew what got my sad up and running, and right out there.

My friends' lives were fun. Parties, clothes, music, last night's homework, and isn't Brad cute, and I don't want to get fat—am I fat? How I wished this could have been me; carefree and cared about. But it wasn't me. I was the really brainy friend amongst that clique of bright girls. I was the one who understood the deep things, whose story about the death penalty had easily won class Essay of the Year. In Year 6.

I read long books, the deep stuff, epic tales, Greek tragedies and famous lives. At fourteen, I read *Exodus* and cried for the refugees. The American Civil War dead in *Across Five Aprils* made that book into my ultimate death notice. I read my birthday gift, *100 Famous Lives*. How noble and sad for Madame Curie to live for science and die poisoned by her own discovery. I worshipped Madame Curie.

Deep down, deep, deep down inside of me, the sad lived forever. I knew it. All beauty will die, and we all become a death notice.

Saturday was a day at home, a day of hopeless helplessness, Sunday I lay low, but on Monday the sanctuary of school welcomed its Dux student back again.

By fifteen there was no more school for me and now, at sixteen, they pumped the tranquillisers out of my stomach after last Friday.

Now I cry for myself.

WHAT'S GOING ON?

What would you rank as the most important factors in Kath's situation? Do you think she is showing a serious mood disorder? If so, why? What do you make of her story?

Some reflections from Kath's story

The first part of Kath's account might suggest adolescent angst: a bright girl, comparing herself to her peers, to some degree lost in adolescence—like Holden Caulfield, the male protagonist in *The Catcher in the Rye*. The middle section of her account moves the centre of gravity. She is sombre and there is a preoccupation with death, which she states has been present prior to her adolescence. Again, mere adolescent angst, or is there something more worrying going on?

That her 'down' mood may not be too severe is suggested by her use of irony, humour, self-deprecation and intelligence. She may be simply a lonely intellectual 'square peg' in a 'round hole' of vacuous, carefree, socialising friends and family members. That there may be more serious cause for concern seems confirmed by her second-last paragraph—this intelligent girl is no longer able to attend school—and finally by her fantasising or rehearsing a drug overdose. For some people, even the last event (imagined or real) might generate polarised responses—that Kath is just 'attention seeking'. So is she 'at risk', or are her closing thoughts merely a harmless melodramatic fantasy?

Kath's account certainly shows prolonged and pervasive sadness. Why does it worsen at weekends? Are schooldays a distraction from whatever has to be faced or endured at weekends? How much reflects temperament, and how much is the context of her environment?

Does Kath have a serious mood disorder? And—as with Leah's situation—how might the determining and contributing issues best be identified? If this was an entry in her personal diary that you had chanced on (as opposed to a Facebook posting) would you have the right to intervene? If so, would you raise your concerns with her directly, or with a family member?

Irrespective of how this piece came to you, should you approach Kath—to check what's going on and to signal support? Or should she be guided immediately to a professional? If she's to see a professional, then who should it be: a GP, a counsellor, a psychiatrist, the local minister? Is the profession of the practitioner central to your decision, or are their interpersonal characteristics more important?

Here is a third scenario to think about. This story was sent to us by Shelley, the mother of a fifteen-year-old boy. She called it 'A Child Dissolves'. Imagine she is a friend you have caught up with after several years. When you ask her how the kids are going Shelley says her entire family has become preoccupied by concerns about their adolescent son, Cameron. Her account traces the corrosive effect of Cameron's disorder on all of them.

I'll start this story by saying that this year has been a really crappy year—crappy in the true sense of the word. Let me introduce myself: my name is Shelley, and I am a happily married (sorry, feel the need to state that upfront) mother of four terrific, energetic and very different children, two boys and two girls, ranging in age from fifteen down to seven. We live in a modest southern suburb of Sydney and all our children attend the local state school, are involved in sport and we are very much your typical suburban family involved with the local community—we coach sporting teams, and volunteer on committees.

Now with the background set, you will get a picture of who we are before I start on our story. Primarily it revolves around our oldest child, Cameron. As all parents will know, when one child is suffering—the whole family suffers. That's not being overdramatic, it's reality. It's like losing the last piece of the jigsaw puzzle: it will never be whole.

The school year started out like most, with new uniforms, books, bags and a great enthusiasm to get to school, see mates, enrol in sport, and find out what teacher they would have for the year. Cam has been fortunate to be in an extension class since Year 7, and this year going into Year 9, he also made this class. It's great to be included in such a class because, for the most part, he was with kids that actually wanted to learn and question things, rather than the kids that would muck up in class or perhaps be the ones that would tease or pick on other students. But it's a double-edged sword, because to be selected to such a class brings with it added stresses—extra assignments and work. And, of course, the high expectations of teachers. We weighed up the pros and cons, and decided that due to Cam's personality and the type of kid he was, this was the environment he was best suited to. Cam has always been a quiet child, not particularly sporty, and has never quite fitted in with the 'in' crowd.

About halfway through term 1 the wheels started to fall off. At first it was just small things, like not wanting to complete homework, or leaving assignments to the last minute (i.e. the night before they were due), nothing really we could put our finger on, but just a general loss of positive attitude when it came to school. At first, as a parent, you do the thing where you say to yourself, 'He's just being fifteen' or 'being a teenager'; we all developed an 'attitude' in our teens. So there were many stressful evenings where we would see me (Mum) on the computer, helping him complete assignments, and cursing under my breath, and trying to instil in him the proper attitude that would get him through Year 9.

A few weeks went past, and the dreaded phone calls started. You know the ones, your mobile rings at 11.30 a.m. and the caller ID states it's your child's school. You answer it with 'Who is it—and what have they done?', and it would inevitably be something that Cam had said or done at school to a teacher or fellow student, and they were 'reporting it' to a parent. The type of behaviour was (even *I* have to admit it) strange—things like keeping a mental 'hit-list' of fellow students that had upset or hurt him in some way; sitting on his own every lunchtime and just listening to his iPod; not engaging in any way in class or, when he did, the comments were inappropriate or not even on the subject; speaking about negative topics, like war and destruction; obsessing on depressing topics like death.

We sought the help of the school counsellor (let's call her Tina, because I don't know if she would like her name to be used), and she agreed that Cam was exhibiting signs of extreme stress, and spoke with him, suggesting ways he could overcome his negative thought processes and the isolation he had put himself into.

Fellow students were not forgiving, and he was alienated and became the butt of jokes on a daily basis. Cam was very shut-down about sharing his thoughts with any of the teachers, and usually just went to school, 'endured' the school day, and made his way home as quickly as he could, only to explode with his family, picking on his younger siblings on a daily basis, and upsetting his father and me constantly—we know now, not purposely, but at the time he was a very difficult child to live with, and we were starting to unravel as a family unit.

The stress that surrounded him on a daily basis was engulfing the entire household, many nights ending in a shouting match with Cam saying the most unforgivable things, and my husband on the phone to my mother for some moral support. We were grasping at straws to understand what was happening, and it was clearly beyond our control or manageability as his parents.

Towards the end of term 1, things were at such a crisis we were forced to seek professional help—there was no alternative. No amount of love or talking to this child was changing things; no amount of 'grounding' or punishing him for his actions was getting through. Each day, the child we knew and loved dissolved a little more. It was confronting, scary and depressing, and left us thinking we had failed as his parents—all the while having another three very impressionable children to parent to the best of our abilities and hope they were not being permanently scarred by this whole affair.

Cam at this stage was almost a completely different person, constantly questioning and arguing every point. Everything was looked at in a negative way—he didn't engage on a positive level with anyone or anything. Even the way he spoke was 'rough' in nature. He chose to escape by staying in his room and playing video games all weekend, or watching movies. We constantly tried to get him to come and eat with us, or go for a visit to a relative's house, but when he did, we found ourselves having to excuse his (strange) behaviour, or explaining it. He would pick arguments with everyone, and appreciated nothing. He needed to be reminded to get up, have a shower. Everything was just too hard. He couldn't be bothered plugging into life. In the end, we didn't want to bring him with us, but were too afraid to leave him behind. He had become a loose cannon—we just could not predict what he would be like. I had headaches that lasted weeks from the stress. Many weekends my husband took the younger three out, and I stayed at home for fear that if I left Cam, he would hurt himself. I was the one that constantly watched him and it was totally exhausting and debilitating.

It got even worse. The negative comments increased and he would say things like 'I hate my life', 'I hate everyone around me'. Getting him out of bed for school each morning was a case of literally dragging his body out of bed and standing there until he started to get dressed. Forcing him to walk to the bus stop. I never knew it could ever be this hard. He was not raised to be this way. Something inside his brain had switched off—his will to be human and live a happy life … or something. Friends constantly complained about what their teenagers were up to, 'staying out late', or 'not coming straight home from the party'. I was mute; give us those problems … Our son hadn't been invited to a party the entire time he had been in high school. He had no friends to socialise with on weekends, and didn't want to go anywhere anyway. They simply had no idea.

WHAT'S GOING ON?

What would you think are the most relevant factors in Cam's psychological deterioration? Do you think it is a serious depression, and if so, why? What are the risks to Cam—and to his family?

Some reflections from Cam's story

This is a description from the outside looking in. You, as a family friend, can have little idea about what Cameron is experiencing. Possibly neither does Cam himself. His mood dysregulation is clearly serious—but is it just 'severe stress', as described by the school counsellor?

Possible determining factors come to your mind. Cam has always been a quiet child and without much outlet from sporting activities. As the oldest of four children, he has shown many of the traits that follow naturally from being the first-born child. As Cam appears to lose his psychological footing, his parents are worried that they might have exposed him to too much stress because they encouraged his extension activities, yet until now these had seemed stimulating and within his grasp.

The onset of puberty is a challenge in itself, and that—coupled with his social withdrawal, and then being marked as a loner and deliberately alienated—has worsened his volatile moods, with anger and negativity erupting to the point where he has become a danger to himself.

His highly concerned mother is reluctant to pathologise the problem, but what if this is a 'primary' mental illness—such as schizophrenia or melancholic depression—that would benefit from urgent medical attention? Or might he be taking illicit drugs without his parents' knowledge … or might they be aware and Shelley is not telling you?

Perhaps there is a family history of mental illness that could clarify the possibilities. But should you ask Shelley that question? And how would you answer that last question if Cameron had the possibility of a *medical* rather than a *psychiatric* problem? If there's a difference, then it is instructive to consider the reasons that caused you to respond differently. (See Chapter 7 for a follow-up of Cam's story.)

These accounts set the backdrop to this book, which seeks to provide a logical framework for how to go about assisting a young person with depression—particularly in seeking out information and relevant professional help to resolve the diagnosis, identify causes and initiate best management strategies. The topic is difficult in itself, and made even more so by the context—the nature of adolescence.

Remember the fable about the blind men and the elephant. In John Godfrey Saxe's version,[1] a blind man feeling the elephant's side judged that it resembled a wall; another, at its tusk, thought it like a spear; a third, feeling the trunk, supposed it snake-like; a fourth, at the elephant's knee, held that it was like a tree; the fifth felt its ear, and believed the elephant to be fan-shaped; and the sixth, at its tail, assumed that it was like a rope … 'Though each was partly in the right, and all were in the wrong!'

The following chapters suggest a way forward, offering guidance to sort through the patterns of teenage distress, and enhanced by the strategies offered by young people who have bested their mood swings.

. . . .

RECOGNISING THE PATTERNS

The following framework can be used as a starting point to help sort through what is happening for a teenager who is troubled.

Is it depression?

Young people may not show obvious signs such as a downcast, non-reactive face that has lost 'the light in the eyes', but they might express their feelings through uncharacteristic behaviours—as described below, and in more detail in Chapter 2.

The range of depression

'Depression' is a word that has become widely used, so its meanings are rather diffuse. While it refers to a cluster of feelings and behaviours that we are generally familiar with, depression can affect an individual as:

- a normal mood state
- a disorder, or
- a physical illness.

'Normal' versus 'clinical' depression

All of us experience 'normal' depression from time to time. It usually comes with some kind of setback in life, and we feel sad and helpless or despairing in response; our self-esteem can suffer too. Such normal states of depression usually have a context, the depressive reaction is in proportion to the event that distressed us—the stressor—and the down mood can be expected to lift and lighten if the stressor is 'neutralised' or ends. The down mood that happens in this case makes sense, both to the teenager and others. And after a short time, the teenager's intrinsic coping skills come into play so that the 'depression' spontaneously improves.

But if a teenager has a clinical depression, differences— while not absolute—exist. The symptoms will persist, with very little let-up over time, and the young person lacks the capacity for spontaneous remission—that is, they can't seem to bounce back to their usual temperament setting. With clinical depression, the teenager's own usual ways of coping are either not working, or are not strong enough to stave off their downward mood spiral, or they don't kick in at all.

Symptoms of clinical depression include:

- a severely depressed mood
- lowered self-esteem
- feelings of worthlessness and a sense that life is not worth living
- irritability and anger.

Other symptoms of clinical depression that impact on a teenager's ability to carry on with life include:

- loss of interest in day-to-day activities
- inability to enjoy or look forward to fun things
- disturbed sleep
- withdrawal and 'cocooning'
- weight change—either up, as they binge on comfort foods, or down, as appetite is lost
- feeling hopeless and helpless, or numb and distant—with these feelings damaging relationships and limiting the ability to function.

Bipolar mood swings

(Previously known as 'manic depressive illness' for more severe states)

Some people have a mood disorder that swings from depression to a quite opposite mood state. People with bipolar disorder generally experience both 'highs' (mania, or hypomania) and 'lows', although a small number only have highs. The lows are almost always 'melancholic' depression (described in more detail in Chapter 5).

During a high, the young person will be elated and feel terrific—although sometimes there is a thread of agitation through the good feeling. Self-esteem is increased; they feel attractive and very confident. They talk more and faster than usual. Their mind races. They have lots of energy and need less sleep. Others can see that their judgment may be poor, and that the person is seeing the world through rose-coloured glasses. Purchases and commitments may be undertaken without due regard for the consequences. Although most teenagers with bipolar disorder feel happy, friendly and amusing, some become irritable and aggressive when high—just as some people who have drunk too much are happy and some are aggressive.

For a teenager on a high, it's as if their brakes have failed. Whatever direction they were going in, they tend to go too far—gambling, shopping, fast driving, arguments, sex, drinking, drugs, showing off …

While some of the world's most creative people have been diagnosed with bipolar disorder, it's an 'asset' with liabilities. If most people have four-cylinder brains, bipolar people have V8s. Unfortunately, they also have cheap drum brakes. A dangerous combination!

Bipolar disorder is thought to be primarily caused by biological factors. It is a disorder that is genetic and strongly inherited, and often begins to manifest in the teenage years.

• •

2. Background stresses
Teenagers shoulder some heavy baggage

Anna's whole childhood was spent tiptoeing around her family and as a result, her self-esteem plunged. When the inevitable tsunami of sadness collided with adolescence, she didn't have the experience of age to know what was really happening. She was just a child unfortunate to be surrounded by so many people with broken records. Nobody cared and she learned very quickly that in her family she didn't matter. She really was the 'waste of space' her father called her. **Anna**

Teenagers' difficulties seem rather different to the problems faced by adults. Young people are still evolving their sense of themselves and others, and of how the world is, and are very open to feedback from the outside. It is as though they are creating their adult carapace or tough outer shell—and until this is formed they are very open and vulnerable to their own experiences and sensations, and to events and individuals around them. Even using our 'retrospectoscopes', we can't readily recapture the heightened emotions of adolescence. Those who kept frank diaries during their adolescence may be surprised, when they read them later in life, by the intensity and life-and-death importance attached to the interactions and events of this time.

DEVELOPMENTAL AND SITUATIONAL CRISES

In psychiatric terminology, adolescence is sometimes thought of as a 'developmental crisis', in that it is associated with heightened emotions, change and pressure to readjust. The teenager must find and define their place in the world. Every young person will experience such issues as they negotiate adolescence. How well they manage each developmental stage leads to a mix of positive, and sometimes negative, outcomes.

Alongside such normal developmental crises are the so-called 'situational crises'. These are reactions to the frustrations produced by particular external—and usually unexpected—events. Examples in a teenager's life might include not achieving their goals in school or sports, the divorce of their parents, being bullied, or the failure of a valued relationship. The way such disappointments and frustrations are managed can shape future attitudes and behaviours.

Other elements in the mix include the teenager's individual 'hard-wired' characteristics: traits such as their vulnerability to anxiety, a tendency to perfectionism, impulsiveness or social reserve and shyness, which can make it more difficult to deal effectively with certain events.

Counsellors generally consider that if these stages of development and crises aren't negotiated, whether because of a young person's personality and/or stressful events, their psychological development may be somewhat arrested or distorted, with longer-term risks to their functioning and wellbeing.

CHRONIC AND ACUTE STRESSORS

Stress is modelled as acute or chronic, or a mix of the two. Acute stress—which can range from exam pressures through to the death of a close friend—can initiate a 'reactive' depression, or an 'adjustment disorder' where the adolescent may go off the rails as they show their distress.

Chronic stress—for example, ongoing pressure to perform at a level that is not within the teenager's abilities; or living with a severely ill and demanding parent—can promote a style of coping known as 'learned helplessness', where the young person is conditioned by circumstances outside his or her control to feel that there is nothing they can do that will have any effect on the outcome of events affecting them, with a consequent loss of their sense of self-efficacy.

Here is one writer's observation about the stressors faced by all teenagers as they move from one developmental stage to another. Add to these the relentless impact of television, internet and being constantly available via mobile phones. For those who develop a mood disorder in their younger years, such stressors can worsen its impact. Here Justin shares some thoughts from his piece, titled 'Baggage'.

A British psychologist, Dr Tim Cantopher of the Priory Clinic,[1] diagnosed the Atlas syndrome, one that has become increasingly relevant to the complexity of modern life. He discovered that many overstressed male Superdads were burdened by the everyday demands of their responsibilities like Atlas, the Titan of Greek mythology whose name was used to describe the illness as he had been forced by Zeus to support the sky on his shoulders. This syndrome is now credited as being not solely suffered by males and some might find it appropriate to use this to sum up the life of an adolescent.

Metaphorically, the modern teenager may be considered to be a bellboy/girl negotiating the course of their lives by carrying baggage that represents the demands of their roles and the environment. For many, this balancing act is easily taken in one's stride; but for some, large amounts of burden can tip them over and make it difficult for them to carry on. Some have used the analogy of a black dog barking at their side or lurking in the shadows to sum up this most painful illness. But this sinister creature can also be represented by a large amount of heavy luggage. I will now examine some of the things that can contribute to the onset of a mood disorder.

Bag 1: Families

There is no denying that families provide endless amounts of inspiration, love, support and nurturing. However, these close relationships, while predominantly positive, can also be the source of negative events such as divorce and the blending of families.

Families can also place pressure on the adolescent, perhaps pressuring them to do well in their final exams, having unrealistic expectations about their future, and even choosing the career for them or making other important decisions without consulting their child. At times the combination of the aforementioned, combined with a genetic predisposition for depression, can spell trouble in the balancing act of life.

Bag 2: Adolescence

Some people say that a change can be as good as a holiday, but this would be an overly simplistic portrayal, ignoring the fact that change can also be a tumultuous experience. Adolescence spells the beginning of puberty and physical growth from childhood to adulthood. Adolescence means mental and physical changes; greater influences are felt from friends and the peer group, including the pressure to experience their first romantic attachments and to experiment with new things. Adolescence can make people feel disempowered as they experience a lack of control when faced with the new and often unexpected. Frequently the black dog of depression will begin to manifest during this occasionally difficult period when their confidence may be lacking and when people around them are lamenting about how their future career and success will depend on the important decisions they make during this time.

Bag 3: The media

Knowledge is power and a far better option than ignorance—and the media serves to keep people informed about the world in which they live. This includes the media reporting on stories about poverty, bigotry, domination, power struggles and other tragedies. Global warming is our legacy to the future generations of this planet. If you stop and think about all of this, it is very easy to feel demoralised, so instead you may choose to look for a media alternative that encompasses some more whimsical subject matter. The only problem is that if you pick up a fashion magazine, your sadness is exacerbated as you feel your insecurities multiply and become more potent. The medium focuses on physical perfection and beauty, materialism and the 'amazing' lives of celebrities—stories that are always far more interesting and eventful than young Chloe studying at Peak Hill High School who can't afford the newest Louis Vuitton handbag with matching pet accessories. Plus, while previously this obsession with body image and sex was confined to adolescence and part of adulthood, now we have the premature sexualisation of youth whereby companies are convincing eight-year-olds that they must have bras and the latest line of sexy underwear. Thus, being an occasionally unwilling audience member of the mass media, if you did not already feel bad, the chances are that your self-confidence is fast dwindling and you feel even more of the world's weight on your shoulders. So you would be forgiven for starting to feel a little sick.

Bag 4: Physical ailments

Now comes the really bad news. Maybe you've just been diagnosed with a serious illness, or possibly someone close to you has. Maybe a family member or friend has recently passed away. It may seem far-fetched, but feelings of grief are natural in these circumstances. Grief felt for others. Grief over your own actual loss or the apparent loss of your healthier self. Stress may accumulate and sadness may begin to feel like the only emotion you will continue to feel in the future—and sometimes only negative emotions seem possible. Therefore, while some grief is a natural part of life, events like this, combined with a vulnerability to depression, can contribute to anyone developing their own black dog. Subsequently, sleep patterns can change. You may become insomniac, or on the flipside, sleep all day but feel tired and lethargic, regardless of the amount of sleep or lack of it. This does not help matters and may lead people towards escapist measures.

Bag 5: Escapism to the virtual world

The modern world is a complicated place. Humans have reality *and* the virtual world to negotiate and it appears that, more and more, people are not content with the reality of their lives, instead seeking another one—one that may include fame, notoriety or the virtual self on the internet. Some people may feel withdrawn and isolated as basic human interaction decreases and life becomes one large popularity contest to see how many friends you have on MySpace or Facebook, or how many contacts you have in your email address book or in your mobile phone. That's not to completely discount these tools, as they can facilitate communication with others and can be extremely useful, but one has to wonder if things were easier and if people were happier when life was simpler and we didn't have all of this technology that was supposed to help us (and is often a hindrance to us).

Bag 6: Escapism by using drugs and alcohol

So you've gone from being a calm and collected individual juggling the various elements of your life to feeling like an extremely flustered bellboy/girl who is about to trip into a deep pit while still trying to sustain the weight of the world on your shoulders. Somehow, this situation often compels people to experiment with illicit drugs and alcohol. Yet the actual remedy couldn't be further from the truth. Illicit drugs and alcohol only serve to exacerbate the depressive condition and people will often abuse these drugs as they build a reliance upon and tolerance to them, leading them on a dark, downwards spiral with potentially dire consequences. **Justin**

MENTAL HEALTH STRESSORS AND STATISTICS

Currently, 14 per cent of children and adolescents in Australia are dealing with mental health problems[2] that are intrusive enough to sap their vitality and cause immeasurable distress, not only to them but to all who love and care for them. Overall, it is estimated that **one in five Australian children aged four to seventeen have significant mental health concerns**.[3] Young adults aged eighteen to 24 years have the highest prevalence of mental disorders of any age group, and in this age group youth suicide is the third most common cause of death.[4] This is not to seek to paint an overly sombre picture and lead to flustered overdiagnosis of depression, but such statistics underline the fact that mental health problems are not imaginary, and they serve to emphasise that it is vital to attend to a young person's experiences and learn from their insights, and to link these with effective ways of recognising and managing mental health problems.

While there is a certain universality to the experience of adolescence, regardless of generation or era, teenagers today are impacted by factors that weren't prevalent a few decades ago—the internet, mass electronic media, mobile phones, global warming and other concerns, premature sexualisation, higher rates of divorce, blended families, 'designer' drugs ... and the list goes on. Peer culture is also tougher: there is internet bullying, the breakdown of community groups, the rise of individualism, and the downsides of affluence. So teenagers and those who care for them really need to be well educated about mood disorders, given that this is the time when such disorders commonly first occur, and contemporary pressures can exacerbate the difficulties.

How can we best provide help and support to those who do need it? So much advice, and so little direction! A teenager battling a mood disorder is likely to display this in a complex way. Parents and other caregivers may be at a loss when faced with the seeming contradictions, barriers and conflicting signals from a young person in distress. Heightened expectations and scrutiny have also put added pressure on parents and caregivers, making many perhaps more tentative and less reliant on their own wisdom and common sense. They may be tolerant of moody behaviour, and too 'understanding' about its many reasons, and might fail to follow up on their teen's very real distress. A source of excellent advice is Michael Carr-Gregg's book, *Surviving Adolescents: The must-have manual for all parents*.[5]

Now consider the following extract from 'Hello Darkness: A Memoir'.

I killed myself once, when I was fourteen. As you can tell, it didn't work, otherwise I wouldn't be writing this, 45 sometimes fabulous and sometimes terrible years later. Wow! Was I one seriously messed kid! From day one I was head and shoulders taller than my peers and precocious, and my parents were emotional barbarians, locked into a maelstrom of frustrations and fears. Family life was fraught with his violence and her madness (she could be pretty violent too). They used me as a weapon against each other, my mother loading me with her paranoia about him, he shouting that her parenting would render me 'useless to anyone'. I grew up with self-defence strategies modelled on their behaviour; a wildly defiant, whirling dervish who took a long time to calm.

Tim was twenty-something, handsome, suave, private school, the sort any girl in her right (or wrong) mind would go ga-ga about. He drove a Mini Minor, but said his 'real car was a Porsche'—he actually did say that, in 1963, and I believed him. But it wouldn't have mattered to me one little bit, because what I loved was the way we talked, about ideas, about books. For the very first time I was having real conversations. I'd thought myself utterly trapped—would never find my way out of that intellectual and cultural desert and had often considered suicide. Even had a lethal dose of Valium stashed, for when I'd really had enough. Y'know how desperate everything is when you're fourteen?

Then, suddenly, Tim opened up a world of possibilities for me. There was one problem. I was fourteen and aware that I was jail-bait, being a convincing nineteen to him and desperate to continue that great conversation. So I told my mother, showed her the Valium and swore her to secrecy, on threat of suicide—that's how dysfunctional our relationship was. But of course she didn't keep her word. Tim and I had arrived home around 1 a.m. that night, were sitting in the car talking quietly, and out she came in hysterics, screaming at him, 'How dare you bring my daughter home this late'—as if it was so unusual—and then the clincher, 'I hope you know she's only fourteen.' Tim said, in a very gentlemanly way, 'Yes, she did tell me.' But my heart sank. I knew I'd never see him again.

That was it for me, total despair, and I'd had just enough alcohol to push me over the edge. I went into my room and waited till she'd gone to bed. Then came out, got water and took every one of those 32 capsules that an irresponsible eighteen-year-old friend had given me. I did not expect to wake up, ever again. I did, of course, in hospital some days later. The registrar came to my bedside and said, 'You selfish child. I spend my life saving people with major health problems who are trying to live. You've the constitution of an ox, but you don't deserve it. You make me sick.' And off he stormed. An early practitioner of Rational Emotive Therapy perhaps? Anyway, it was probably the best thing he could have done. **Susan**

BOUNDARY RIDING—BE VIGILANT

While there are diagnostic guidelines that set out the length of time that a mood disorder—such as depression—should be present before it is seen as persistent enough to need assessment, the boundary line between normal sadness and clinical depression is not absolute. The parameters outlined throughout this book are guidelines only. There is a minimum time—two weeks—before a mood disorder such as depression is considered clinical and thus likely to need assessment. But such guidelines should not always be taken literally. The severity of the depression and its impact on the teenager are the most important considerations when you are weighing up whether to become more involved.

A mother of a teenager with severe depression developed these informal questions to help her decide when to intervene. (The teenager has since recovered and is now doing well.)

Ask yourself on a scale of 1–10 how you would rate your teenager:

- How bad (in all sorts of ways) are they?
- Are they 'themselves' or not?
- What impact is their mood state/behaviour having on their life?
- Are you worried about them not coping?

The onset of a depression can be sudden and devastating, even if it has been present for only a few hours or days. **An adolescent might develop a severe depression and be at risk of suicide in a matter of hours**—for instance, as an acute reaction following a rejection in a relationship. A response of deep sadness to such an event makes sense. And even if it has only been present for a brief period, such an individual may still be at risk, and will be highly responsive to either poor advice or wise counselling—with their distinctly different outcomes.

Your gut feeling, instinct and common sense come into play. You know how your child once was, and if you feel they might be at risk, arranging an assessment by a professional definitely trumps holding back and waiting for fear of invading the young person's space.

Similarly, you may have been worriedly watching a teenager who has been showing considerable distress and/or withdrawal, and then notice that suddenly they seem relieved and the situation appears to be resolved. This may, paradoxically, be a cause for increased concern rather than comfort. The young person's mood of calm resolution and newly acquired peacefulness can sometimes presage a dramatic solution. (Please see Appendix II: Assessing the risk of harm in teenagers with depression.)

This next extract is from a girl, now adult, who carried burdens that nearly became too heavy for her to bear. It is moving to see how much courage she musters and how her humanity enables her to reframe her past without bitterness. She called her story 'Permission'.

At night, late, through the door, she used to hear her mother's voice. Its cutting harsh tones, the savagery, the biting sarcasm. Her father didn't fight back.

'Why do you say such things?' he asked. 'I wish you wouldn't.'

By day, it was obvious why she said such things.

The verandah rotted into grey splintery shards. Through the gaps a blue-tongue lizard poked its head to regard the family with an impassive reptilian stare. In biology she learnt that the lizard had been there since the Mesozoic Era some 250 million years ago and thus, one blink of its heavy lid symbolised the period of their entire tenure on that decaying farm.

The lizard didn't get out of her way and she knew she was nothing. She had to jump over it.

Nobody bothered to collect the fruit, which her mother used to preserve in jars kept on a kitchen shelf: rows of glowing golden peaches, ruby plums, apple jelly. That year the fruit lay under the trees shrivelling in the heat, browning and bursting, stinking like old sweet wine. Magpies paused from gorging on the feast and looked at her with the same age-old scathing reptilian stare of the lizard. In their dusty yards the hens panted and waited for her to tip buckets of wheat across the barren pebbly grey earth. Their eyes too expressed only hard scorn and greed.

In his careful meticulous hand her father recorded the arithmetic of all this in a big accounting ledger. Columns of black and red. At the end of that summer he told their man, Tom, that they could not afford him anymore and he'd have to go. She learnt of this only when she passed Tom on the road from the house averting his wet cheeks and muttering an incoherent farewell.

Men came and, like the lizard and the magpie, they stared inscrutably at her before going out to tot up the value of the family's assets in their own competing ledgers.

At the auction her parents ignored proceedings and kept inside the house, but she roamed amongst the buyers and the neighbours and the Saturday curious and watched the auctioneer move briskly from one poor pile of machinery to another of galvanised iron and another of livestock. Reduced to lots, her family's foundations, as it seemed, crushed to dust under the repetitive blows of his hammer.

The family moved to a small suburban house, packed amid a hundred such suburban brick villas. For the first time she saw her father lose his temper. He threw a newspaper at her; she'd walked for miles but hadn't managed to buy him the correct edition. One day she surprised him drinking brandy from a bottle in heavy gulps. Each afternoon, after school, he waited for her to bring him news of her day. The interrogation became more and more intrusive and she took to slipping into her room by the back door and avoiding her parents altogether. She become obsessed with quadratic equations and learnt *Macbeth* and *Julius Caesar* off by heart, and turned that dead language, Latin, into English prose her teacher loved.

Her cousin, the doctor, visited and her father showed him the strange, apricot-sized lumps that had grown along his neck, over the right collarbone. The cousin said he didn't know what they were and did not come back.

Shortly after that her father took to his bed. One day she passed his bedroom door and saw him playing with his penis and mewling like a baby. Her mother's neglect was blatant. She treated him like a whingeing preschooler.

During the long school holidays, meticulously, she built a ship from plastic parts and spent hours reproducing the rigging exactly from the thick black cotton supplied by the manufacturer. An Airfix model. Airfix made fighter planes also. The Spitfire seemed the most beautiful aeroplane ever made. Built for attack and rapid flight. Escape.

One very hot day in mid-summer an ambulance came and two discordantly lively men moved her father onto a stretcher, carried him out of the house and deposited him on the footpath whilst somebody manoeuvred their vehicle closer. He gazed at the sky in bewilderment. A group of neighbours gathered and watched this now brown stick creature lie on the ground with his face full of childish pain and innocence. She wanted to kill all of them. That is a good man and you don't know him, was what she felt. How dare you gawp.

She was physically unable to walk across the street to attend his funeral service.

Her mother wept for weeks after that. She did too. But she knew her mother's tears sprang from guilt, as did her own, and she thought that a death shouldn't have been allowed to happen like that and it was her mother's fault.

As she had promised her father, she dutifully went to university and entered the faculty of his choice, not her own.

One night she informed her mother that she would no longer eat dessert and the last dessert which her mother made her lay on the table for hours: an apple pie sinking into congealing custard. By bedtime the custard had formed a yellow shroud over the brown sticks of crust.

Soon she found she could live on one apple a day. She walked for miles. Occasionally she passed a shop-stand full of loaves of crusty brown bread and she saw herself ripping them out of their plastic wrapping and pushing her nose and face into the warm odour of yeasty food and gorging herself. But she didn't. With 30 kilograms lost very quickly she felt as though she could control the world.

Sleep was hard to come by and now and then she hammered on the floor with her fists because she was so angry. At what, she didn't know. The anger was a terrific pressure in her brain. It had no direction. She and her mother barely acknowledged each other. Her mother 'took to drink', as the saying goes.

As her periods had, by now, stopped altogether she obeyed her mother's instructions and went to a GP, who found nothing wrong, but gave her the contraceptive pill to restart them. To give her due credit, the GP had briefly asked her if she was really happy in her field at university. She lied and said that of course she was. She had kept passing, hadn't she?

One night, out of curiosity and because she was always thinking of killing herself in an abstract way, which had been, until then, just words in her head, she drew a razor across both wrists and watched the blood well up. It was such a satisfactory sight, such a satisfactory feeling, that she was surprised at her pleasure. The pull of debasement and self-pity shocked her and she made a vow never to attempt such a thing again unless she really meant to kill herself and, in that case, she should do it correctly, carefully and successfully. That had been the way her father had conducted his life. It was a proper way to run a life: to make decisions and follow them through creatively, perfectly, surely.

A record company sent her monthly music. She played Beethoven's *Sixth Symphony* over and over and over. And over. There was message of strife and reconciliation. Storms which pass. Something to do with the nature of life and the connection of human beings in their unavoidable suffering. Bach later seemed to be saying the same thing.

Then a therapist said, '*You don't need to feel like this anymore.*'

What an extraordinary gift that was. Permission to stop 'doing time' for her father's suffering and lonely death. That was the day she stopped feeling she was special because she was thinking of suicide every day, and special because she had suffered, and special because she had passed every damn exam in a faculty she really thought was skimpy on certitude and big on hubris.

Now she listens to Bach and Archie Roach and knows her suffering is as nothing. Her father was a good man and she was lucky to have known him. There are others just like him. Not all women carry her mother's bitterness around to ferment bad fortune into a life's curse, like rotting fruit on the ground. Not everybody views life with the cold impassive gaze of a lizard.

And the lizard has no knowledge of the stars. **Trudy**

In addition to helping Trudy unburden herself and validating her experiences, the therapist in the account above gave her a tool that was missing from her coping kit: permission. This permission enabled Trudy to cease blaming herself for events that were always outside her control. She was freed to re-examine and reframe the past, and to see it more realistically. This permission helped her to heal and to view herself more positively.

Most young people, apart from predictable stumbles, make their way through the thickets of the teenage years—as did we. Adolescents are a powerhouse of ideas and ideals; they refresh our perspectives. They have much in them that is strong and healthy, energetic, inventive and resilient. Fortunately, they are not often required to undertake psychological marathons but sometimes circumstances and/or their own personal characteristics mean that they require support over some hurdles.

WHEN IN DOUBT …

The severity of a teenager's depression and its impact upon them are the most important factors to consider, rather than whether a mood disorder is a 'clinical' condition or not. The real question to ask yourself is 'Would this teenager benefit from an assessment?' as opposed to 'Does this adolescent require treatment?' It is the task of the assessor to determine if—and what—treatment and management might be beneficial.

'If in doubt, talk it out' and arrange an assessment by an appropriate and competent professional. Different aspects of assessment are considered in Chapter 4.

. . . .

RECOGNISING THE PATTERNS

Here is a more detailed outline of depression and bipolar disorder, which were briefly introduced towards the end of Chapter 1.

What is 'depression'?

Depression is a mood state where there is a drop in self-esteem and sense of self-worth, where the individual feels 'down' and pessimistic and wants to give up, and feels others have given up on them too. It can be a 'normal' mood state (akin to sadness), a severe reaction to stressors, or a disease state (such as melancholic, psychotic or bipolar depression).

How is depression different to grief and anxiety?

The defining characteristic of **depression**, and what sets it apart from anxiety and grief, is lowered self-esteem.

In **anxiety**, the main feeling is of insecurity. Anxiety is experienced either as quite general (or 'free-floating'), or it can be tied to some particularly feared situation.

Grief is the pain we experience at the loss of someone or something highly valued by us. However, grief is not associated with loss of self-esteem.

How is depression related to grief and anxiety?

Though different, depression can be closely associated with anxiety and grief in the following ways:

- as anxiety increases, so does the chance of depression
- a third of people who have experienced major grief and loss will go on to feel depressed
- for those who develop clinical depression, there is an increased chance of anxiety—shown in features like worrying and rumination (negatively mulling repeatedly over past situations), or presenting in other forms, like panic attacks.

Signs and symptoms of depression

Depression can be signalled in teenagers by one or more of the following signs and symptoms:

- becoming asocial—avoiding school and friends, and not returning phone calls and text messages from friends
- poorer school performance, both in class and sports
- heightened irritability, anger, hostile outbursts

- indecisiveness
- lack of energy and motivation
- restlessness, agitation, disruptive behaviours, overactivity
- loss of pleasure and interest in activities
- a sense of hopelessness or pessimism about the future
- increased sensitivity to failure or rejection; highly self-critical
- feelings of guilt and worthlessness—a sense of needing to be punished
- a helpless inability to change the way they feel
- complaints of headaches, stomach aches, tiredness, 'growing pains'
- persistent sadness and bouts of crying
- morbid thoughts and statements (direct and indirect), such as they feel worthless or don't want to continue living
- deliberate self-harm
- risk-taking (for instance, inappropriate sexual contacts, reckless driving)
- drug and alcohol abuse
- changes in eating and sleeping patterns (too much or too little)
- uncharacteristic behaviours, such as stealing and bullying.

Of course, none of these features are specific to depression alone, as they may have other causes. Nor are they all necessarily 'pathological'. Issues such as how specific a symptom or sign is to a particular disorder and how its severity is measured will be addressed later in the book.

What 'type' of depression is it?

As noted in Chapter 1, depression can be normal or pathological ('clinical'), with the latter being more severe and persistent and more likely to show increasing numbers of the features listed above.

Episodes of clinical depression may be **melancholic** (a more 'biological' disorder) or **non-melancholic** (a less 'pure' type of depression that arises as a result of one or more stressors interacting with the individual's personality style).

Individuals may also have different 'shapes' to their depression: there may be episodes of clinical depression solely (a unipolar pattern), or episodes of clinical depression oscillating with hypomania or mania (a bipolar pattern).

Bipolar mood swings

Extreme 'ups', or elevations in mood that interfere with everyday life, may signal bipolar disorder. Some of the signs and symptoms during highs include:

- acting 'wired' and energised
- excessive sensitivity to sensory input
- losing normal anxieties and feeling carefree
- needing less sleep, but not feeling tired (initially)
- 'pressured' speech and racing thoughts
- talking more—often loudly and over people
- having 'grand scheme' ideas
- frequent, rapid and dramatic changes in mood
- becoming overly frank and disinhibited (e.g. verbally, sexually)
- feeling creative, spiritual, mystical, at one with nature
- spending more money—often buying unaffordable items
- being irritable and impatient, easily frustrated, or having severe temper tantrums
- fuelling the highs with alcohol and drugs to go even higher
- poor impulse control
- an increase in impulsive and risk-taking behaviours.

Along with these highs, the person may also experience alternating episodes of **melancholic** or even **psychotic** depression. The features of these are further detailed in Chapter 5.

What type of bipolar disorder is it?
Most commonly, bipolar disorder is either Type I, involving psychotic manic episodes, or Type II, featuring non-psychotic hypomanic episodes. However, 'pseudo-highs' can be induced in some people merely by starting an antidepressant, or by increasing its dose or ceasing it altogether (so-called Bipolar III).

What causes depression—clinical or otherwise?

Many factors can predispose, precipitate or perpetuate mood disorders. They include:

- a genetic loading—it may run in the family
- traits such as high anxiety, and certain personality styles, which can make someone more susceptible to developing a depressive episode
- medical problems which may cause the adolescent to feel depressed (such as severe diabetes), and/or which might impact on brain functioning to cause depression (such as multiple sclerosis)
- low levels of self-esteem, and factors lowering self-esteem throughout childhood and adolescence, such as lack of parental care, parental overprotection, bullying
- any major developmental stressors—for instance, sexual abuse, disability, injury
- grief due to death, injury or illness of another
- threats to an individual's stability, such as parental absence, illness, disharmony or divorce, or frequent moves of school
- problems with peers, such as bullying or the break-up of a close peer relationship

- being burdened with too much pressure, or overly high expectations
- lack of social stimulation; poverty, disadvantage
- difficulties arising from differences in cultural background
- drugs—both prescribed drugs that may cause depression, as well as all illicit drugs (including steroids)
- guilt issues, such as problems with sexual identity
- body image problems—and any eating disorder, declared or hidden
- physical problems, such as lack of sleep
- environmental stressors, such as a change of seasons, changing time zones, disruptions to the circadian rhythm (see Glossary)
- any significant financial pressure and its cause, such as compulsive gambling.

Some of these factors are also implicated in the development of bipolar disorder—in particular, genetic loading, sleep disruption, and environmental pressures that impact on circadian rhythm.

Is the mood disorder 'primary' or 'secondary'?

A mood disorder is classed as primary if it is considered to be the principal or sole condition, for any of the following reasons:

- it is the main problem troubling an individual, so success-fully treating the disorder should relieve any other secondary problems they are having
- of all the other problems faced by the individual, it is having the greatest damaging effect
- it was the first destabilising factor, which then led to a series of secondary problems. For example, a young person

getting along well at school develops a primary biological depression, and then becomes ostracised and bullied because of withdrawal and irritability; the ostracism and bullying are now underpinning their current loss of self-esteem, even though the primary depression may have been brought under control.

A secondary mood disorder follows on from—and is essentially the consequence of—a primary psychiatric disorder (for instance an anxiety disorder, or attention deficit hyperactivity disorder), a primary medical condition (such as epilepsy or head injury), or another primary cause, such as alcohol or drug abuse.

. . . .

How mood disorders can be classified and subdivided
This diagram shows the need to first distinguish depression and bipolar disorder from other disorders, and then how mood disorders can be subdivided.

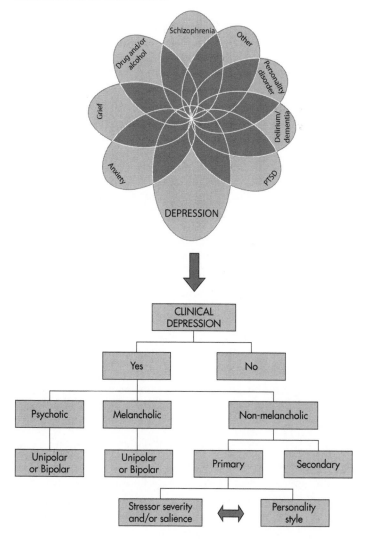

3. What depression feels like
Young people describe its effects

The screams rise from the pit of his stomach, like bees
freed from a jar. **Josh**

Everything changed two months into his first year of high
school. He stopped talking, laughing, singing. He moved
in and out of rooms like a spectre, slumping against
life. Our happy home became a prison; he, a nebulous
version of his former self, locked behind the bars of his
mind. I looked for clues but his eyes were empty discs
hyphenated by deep stress lines of an emotional pain
too great for one so young. **Liza**

The actual experience of depression—how it is to live through
it—has been effectively portrayed by writers such as William
Styron and Kay Redfield Jamison. They have been generous
in putting aside their own privacy to reveal the horror and
sometimes (black) humour of depression and bipolar disorder.
A more recent book by Michael Greenberg describes his
daughter's illness (in retrospect, and with her encouragement)
as it struck their family one summer.[1]

The following excerpts illustrate how teenagers are often
just as confused as those around them by what is happening
to them. The accounts underline the toxic blockage enforced

by a 'silent' mood disorder. The young person seems derailed from the energetic questing of their peers and paralysed in a painful limbo. It is a dangerous place to be, and it can leave lifelong scars.

In this chapter, we move to the inner world of depression and how it manifests in multi-faceted ways. So many factors— both internal and external to the young person—can shape the clinical picture. Before we explore the logic of how to approach mood swings and negotiate that maze without losing your bearings, here are some brief accounts of how a mood disorder *feels*. Understanding the isolation and despair it engenders may persuade carers to seek an assessment for a teenager they can sense is troubled.

This boy—now an adult—was unaware that what he felt was common, so then, understanding that he might be not quite right, he was unable to frame what was wrong.

First, I had to be aware there was even a problem. Awareness is the first step to living a life with a mood disorder. Constant anxiety and excessive self-criticism are not normal, as expressed in the typical subtitles that would scroll through my mind: 'They think I'm stupid/ugly/weird … They don't like me … I'm not good enough … I wish I were more like her … They're staring at me … there must be something wrong with me … I'll be alone for the rest of my life …' I was unaware that the emotions I was experiencing and the way it was affecting my ability to lead a fulfilling life was actually something that many people were struggling with and that there was help available.

After the saga of high school, while moping about in my room one day, my ears tuned in to an interview with actor Garry McDonald: '… mind … race off in its negativity, to bring you down all the time ... not good enough ... wake up in the morning in this just dreadful, dreadful fog ... sitting like this all the time ... it saps you of energy.'[2] Who was this? Those were *my* thoughts. It was due to this experience, knowing other people tormented themselves, that I knew that I might not be 'quite right'. To be aware there is a problem is one thing, to pin it down with a label is something else. **Nathan**

This adolescent girl presses on through her distress, unaware that this isn't how it has to be. She adopts a mask of being in control in order to function.

I thought this was just the way it was, to be always struggling to stay on top of my feelings of desolation. The years of my childhood passed by and when puberty occurred it brought with it a strong feeling of darkness that cascaded all around me, engulfing me in its cruel force. I felt empty, hollow, irritable and alone. My heart felt as though it could split open into two empty halves as sadness invaded me.

I went through the mundane tasks of daily living—trying to appear calm, collected, strong and in control of my life. It was not until I climbed into bed at night that I was able to drop this mask and facade. Friendships, relationships and my social life were restricted, limited and affected as a result of my ongoing flat and down mood. At its darkest I would pull out of social gatherings with friends as I knew I would be unable to function and communicate with them effectively. The haze of darkness surrounded me and it strengthened throughout my teenage years. **Poppy**

Another young woman struggles on in isolation, unaware that she is not alone with her problems. She probably put on too good a front for those around her to notice that anything was amiss, so she was not guided towards any sources of support. Looking back, she reflects that this time of untreated depression had an impact on her future, limiting her opportunities.

I was unaware that the emotions I was experiencing were actually something that others struggled with too. My experience of childhood trauma—early-onset depression—sucked the hope out of a prosperous and happy future. And throughout high school my needs for support were not met. As I began experiencing a sense of deep sadness, despair, anxiety and self-hatred, I lacked the skills to address and placate them.

Surprisingly, a private girls school that claimed to meet every young woman's needs lacked the resources to educate students through what is a transformative yet difficult time of development. Hence, I was unaware that the emotions I was experiencing and the way it was affecting my ability to lead a fulfilling life was actually something that many people were struggling with and that there was help available.

It seemed natural to be withdrawing from friends, having sick days, feeling repulsed by my reflection in the mirror. I was unable to articulate it to myself and struggled to write sentences, let alone essays, and sleep and eating became excessive. The percussion I was learning to play drummed to a monotonous beat, and my lust for literature and the arts dissipated overnight. How does a person recognise that their life is slowly being swallowed by quicksand when they have no means to objectively see it happening? How do you seek help when nothing is suggesting that what you are going through could be different?

Only when I googled 'Depression' did I feel a slight sense of relief. **Jasmine**

This boy copes in a way that is not unusual in adolescence—by invoking a litany of physical illnesses. He 'somatises'—channelling his unhappiness through his body. It is quite an effective temporary mechanism if it buys some 'time out', and also provides an acceptable way to experience something as intangible as depression.

> I processed episodes of being stressed out as physical illnesses. My trademark saying, my life-line out, was 'I don't feel so well'. If I had a dollar for every time those words came from my mouth I'd be a very wealthy boy, very wealthy indeed. They had become the only words I needed to speak to let others know … I need a moment, maybe several moments strung together, maybe several weeks strung together, where I have to be accorded some more time, some more patience, some more understanding. **Luke**

The following excerpt illustrates the 'physical' impact of a psychological disorder.

> The ocean seemed to help. I sat on the sand watching the waves rolling in and out, watching the sea take whatever it wanted and only giving back what it felt like. But bending down to tie the laces on my running shoes above the beach one day, I felt a pain under my ribs on the left side of my chest. More diffuse than a stitch, this was painful enough to make me put my hand under my shirt and my palm across my ribs. I pulled it out after a minute or so and looked at it as if there should have been something there, but there was nothing. I was surprised but didn't know why. A while later I realised: it was almost as though my heart was actually bleeding through my chest. I had been looking for blood. **Mick**

This sixteen-year-old girl is still coping with the consequences of her first manic episode and the pain and embarrassment that it brought. Unwitting self-exposure at any age is painful, but during the adolescent years it is particularly excoriating.

Looking back on my behaviour during my manic phase and its treatment makes me embarrassed, and I wish it hadn't happened.

Things started to become seriously wrong with me in March on a school excursion to the Adelaide Music Festival. We had a 24-hour train journey and I didn't get much sleep, if any. And while we were in Adelaide I still got very little sleep; about two hours a night. I had snoring roommates, too, and I tried to escape this by sleeping on the floor in the ladies toilets. I began to get hypomanic. I was having a great time laughing at everything, even things that weren't funny, and talking non-stop. I did realise something was wrong but I had no idea what it was.

After I returned home I was taken to a GP and then to a psychiatrist to try to sort out what was wrong. I was diagnosed with manic depressive illness (or bipolar disorder as it is now known) and started on medications. I became more manic. I tried to stay at school but, in the process, when I was manic, I publicly humiliated myself on several occasions. I ran about 7 km barefoot to school one day and attempted to try out for the boys' second-grade soccer team. I planned to do a striptease in my English class. This was prevented but I still read embarrassing poetry to my class. I also took off my shoes and untucked my shirt and gave books to the school principal in the middle of when I was supposed to be playing my violin at a school music concert. At the time I wasn't embarrassed by any of this, but looking back at it now makes me feel embarrassed and I wish it hadn't happened. On one occasion I also thought I was the Messiah come again. **Emily**

This next account is from a girl who, despite the scepticism and criticism of many of her peers, stuck by her ideals. Initially, such beliefs probably protected her from her encroaching mood swings, but soon these swept all before them and left her exposed to the 'polar winds' and the subsequent shattering of her beliefs.

I needed help, but where could I seek shelter? In my early teens I chose to take the road less travelled. I joined the minority of young people who take life, and in particular faith, seriously. I resisted considerable pressure to conform. Soon, however, the pressure became too much. My mind filled with negative thoughts, constantly churning and worrying what people thought of me. Teenagers can be incredibly cruel in the insensitive way they treat those who dare to be different. The end of high school was a great release.

Self-discovery, I realised, was acceptable in the adult world. Returning to study I met some very unique individuals, as diverse as their hairstyles. They, like me, were explorers. Joining a Christian group at university, I discovered the energy and strength gained from mixing with those with similar passions. I became more and more involved, joining the committee and participating in every social activity. Soon I began to tire, but I did not want to stop.

My mother, experienced at helping people with depression, warned me to slow down. I was becoming irritable, choosing time with friends at the expense of family, study and rest. There was also a heightened sense of spirituality, something I have since discovered to be a symptom of bipolar disorder.

Meanwhile, with more meetings and social gatherings, the tension increased. A rubber band was being wound up inside me. Like a rubber-band-powered model aeroplane, I was so tightly wound that I was unable to release the tension. Knots upon knots. Nothing could stop the winding. Finally the rubber band inside me did the only possible thing it could: it snapped.

The jaws of the black dog snapped shut and I could not shake myself free. Waves of depressing thoughts pounded my crumbling mind. One day I found myself on the floor with my family gathered around me.

I lay on my bed for days, often weeping uncontrollably. My life to me was like a building. It was made up of random building materials: the ideas, thoughts and philosophies of others, but unlike the mansion I had hoped for, it was a shack! For the first time I saw an alternative. I would build a house with new materials, forged in the furnace of personal experience, while salvaging some materials from the old shack. I knew that somehow the new house could withstand the buffeting of the icy polar winds that were swirling around me. In the meantime I needed help, but where could I seek shelter? **Natasha**

Our next writer was stymied. Phoebe has suffered from depression since early childhood, yet could never make sense of her abnormally 'down' feelings. Neither she nor her family could uncover an explanation for her overwhelming and continuous sadness, while her search for an external reason added to her anger and guilt. Her depression—eventually identified as likely to reflect a chemical imbalance—had all the hallmarks of a melancholic, biological depression that for all too long distressed and perplexed her. She called her essay 'My Depression from Nowhere'.

I have suffered from some sort of mood disorder since childhood. However, it has only been in the last five years that I was diagnosed with depression. Depression and other mood disorders can have numerous causes and starting points. Often a traumatic experience can lead to a person feeling depressed, having mood swings, becoming angry and even violent.

In my case, depression seemed to come out of nowhere. I have always had the best friends, a fantastic, loving family and a great education. My only traumatic experience was the 2003 Canberra bushfires. The bushfires added to my anxieties; however, my mood troubles began well before that.

At age five or six, I was crying most nights before I went to bed. I remember being asked why I was crying or what was wrong and having no answer. I even saw the school counsellor. In the end, the counsellor and my parents decided I must just hate school, and was crying because I didn't want to go the next day.

In my early teens I was very low much of the time. I felt like there was always a dark cloud over my head. I had extremely low energy all the time and always felt tired. However, since my moods were brushed off the first time, I figured it would be useless to try to seek help. So I continued to have days when I would feel so awful I could not get out of bed, afternoons when I would come home from school and lie on the couch watching television, and nights when I would lie in bed crying for hours.

Having no apparent reasons for my almost constant low moods was very hard to deal with. I would even get very angry because I was feeling like I had no reason to be upset. I'd always lie and say I was fine rather than trying to explain that I was upset for no reason whatsoever. I felt embarrassed to have these feelings and not know why they were there.

When there is a reason for feeling depressed, such as a break-up or a death, this reason can be sorted through and dealt with. When there is no cause for these feelings, there is nothing that can be done to try to solve them. Every time I felt low and depressed for no reason I would add to it by thinking things like 'I should not be feeling this way'. Especially when my parents and friends were so supportive, I just felt I should not be unhappy. It even got to the point where when something truly sad happened, I would actually be grateful for a reason to be upset because I could deal with what was making me unhappy.

I felt incredibly alone, and to try to feel better I sought help and advice from other teenagers in places like group therapy and internet forums for those suffering from mood disorders. Unfortunately, everyone I spoke to had had some sort of life-changing and/or traumatic experience in their lives. I couldn't seem to find anybody who had the same awful feelings I did for no reason. I felt like this just alienated me further from my peers.

This caused me to become very critical of myself. I was frequently telling myself to 'stop being so stupid' and that I had 'no reason for being upset'. I even accused myself of making it all up or trying to get attention. If there is nothing wrong with my life, then I should not be unhappy, right?

Being so critical of myself led to me hating myself, and this led to self-harm. In my second year of high school I started to cut my legs. My self-harm then spread to my arms and wrists. I had never heard of anyone else doing this to themself, so I had no idea I was even doing anything wrong. I didn't even know that what I was doing had a name! All I knew was that when

I cut myself, I didn't feel all the emotional pain anymore. All I could concentrate on at the time was the injuries I had created. So for a while, I felt like things were better; I had a way to control my emotional pain. However, I then started to use self-harm as punishment as well. If I got upset for no reason, then I felt I had to cut myself as punishment. I began to realise that none of my friends had scratches and other injuries like I did, and started to feel that maybe what I was doing wasn't entirely healthy. But I did not want to give it up, so I made up excuses so my friends wouldn't find out what I was doing.

When my friends realised that all my 'accidental injuries' were indeed self-inflicted, and my cat was in fact sweet and did not scratch me almost every day (as per the excuse I used), they were so scared and begged me to see our high school counsellor. I still saw no problem with what I was doing so I went along with their plan so they would stop asking me if I was okay. I sat in the counsellor's office and listened as my friends went on about how worried they were and how they could not believe I could hurt myself like this. I could see they were all quite distressed and I felt so bad about scaring them. We all cried and hugged, and it was decided I would never harm myself again, and I was to talk to my friends whenever I got sad.

A few days later, my mum sat me down for a chat. The school counsellor had phoned her and told her everything. I felt so completely betrayed, felt like I could not trust anyone. I shut down completely and did not talk to anyone, no matter how bad I felt. I obviously could not trust that counsellor, so I was not even able to talk to *her*. Things with my mum were tense and we did not talk much for a while. My parents, like my friends, did not understand why I would want to hurt myself, and therefore did not know what to say to me about my self-harming. I just brushed it off, said it was nothing and, under my parents' assumption I was no longer harming, it became a bit of a dead issue and we just did not talk about it anymore.

When I finally realised I was not able to deal with my moods by myself, and that I really wanted to hurt myself, I told my parents just how bad I was feeling and agreed to see a doctor. Relief flooded through me as my doctor told me that what I was feeling was quite common and certainly not wrong. She said I have a chemical imbalance in my brain, that sometimes my brain just doesn't produce the same hormones and endorphins as a normal human brain should. After feeling depressed for so many years, it felt great to know why.

Over the years since then I have been seeing a psychologist to learn better ways to deal with moods. I engage in regular exercise and try to be with my friends as much as I can. Being given a rationale for my feelings certainly did not suddenly make everything better. It did, however, make me feel a bit more normal. I have since found other adolescents who suffer from the same sort of chemical imbalance as I do, which helps me to feel less alone. My moods have definitely improved and, best of all, I have now been self-harm-free for five months. **Phoebe**

THE BENEFITS OF ASSESSMENT

In each of the accounts above, the young person would have benefited from independent—including professional—assessment of what was happening for them. The teenage years are a time when an individual forms a lasting sense of themselves and being forced to construct a self-image from perceptions that have been twisted and warped by a persistent mood disorder often leads to 'unpicking' and reconstruction of the 'self' in later years. Also, mood disorders can be notoriously recurrent, and good early management can help to restrain relapse.

As this writer says:

> Not all teenagers are slaves to their wildly fluctuating moods; in fact not all teenagers experience 'moods'. However, in these 'troubled' teens the first signs of depression permeate into their lives gradually, before being detected, much like a termite population devouring the foundations of a home. The ensuing struggle to rid the home of the infestation is a battle which, if fought without professional assistance, one is severely unlikely to win easily. And the later the battle is left, the more the damage. **Jason**

. . . .

A FRAMEWORK FOR ACTION

It is important to realise that there are a wide range of health care professionals who can help assess mood disorders in the teenage years.

Who can help?

It is generally best to seek out a professional who is experienced in dealing with younger people and their problems. You can list suggestions from your GP and from other people you trust. Websites provide variable information and some also carry lists of therapists and their areas of expertise—however, not everyone who puts themselves forward for such listing is necessarily skilled.

Don't be afraid to discontinue contact with a therapist if they don't inspire confidence—either initially or over time. Remember that there may be a certain amount of awkwardness early on, as the areas the therapist will be exploring with your teenager are private and may be painful, so you should allow everyone some time to become comfortable with each other. However, first impressions can be a strong indicator of the therapist's individual characteristics.

Assessment is available from the following health care professionals, although this is not an exhaustive list.

Counsellors

A range of counselling services are available.

- A **guidance officer** or **school counsellor** is a person—often a former teacher—who has been trained to support adolescents through their various problems. Your child doesn't need a parent's or teacher's permission to see them.
- If the young person has left school and is attending a tertiary educational institution, they can see a counsellor provided by the **student health service**.
- A counsellor may be available through your **local church** or **ethnic community group**. It is best to consult someone who is experienced in dealing with teenagers.
- A **family therapist** can be particularly relevant if you feel that some or all of the family would benefit from a discussion, or that the depression is a consequence of major family problems.
- Other therapists also specialise in particular psychological disciplines, such as cognitive behavioural therapy, family therapy, interpersonal therapy, relaxation therapy and hypnotherapy.
- **Social workers** also specialise in mental health.

Clinical services

Many avenues for assessment exist within the medical community.

- A wise **family GP** may provide a gentle point of entry to help, either by offering their own assessment, or by referring the teenager to someone they know has expertise in this area.
- There may be a **psychologist** or **social worker** available in your GP's practice. These professionals sometimes arrange a joint interview together with your doctor to enable a comprehensive assessment.
- A **psychologist** or **clinical psychologist**. These people work in both the public and private health systems. They can meet with a teen to develop a treatment plan. A clinical psychologist has more years of specialist training than a generic psychologist, but the best guide is a warm recommendation from a satisfied 'customer'.
- Your GP may refer the young person for special assessment and treatment by a **psychiatrist**—a medical doctor who has additional qualifications in diagnosing and treating mental health problems. In contrast to psychologists, psychiatrists can also prescribe medication if they assess that it will help.
- A **psychotherapist** will often focus less on the 'behavioural' side of the teenager's distress and more on past history and stresses, depending on the main cause of the problem.
- **Private hospitals** and **psychiatric clinics** have a range of professionals available for consultation. They may also offer education programs and support groups.
- A **psychiatric nurse** may also run support groups— of benefit to some adolescents—as well as support and information groups for carers.
- An **occupational therapist** can help schedule activities to assist rehabilitation and return to normal functioning.
- The local hospital **emergency service** can provide assessment in an emergency. It is, of course, much better if this option is avoided through early recognition of a mood disorder.

There are also emergency telephone counselling services, such as Lifeline (phone 13 11 14). Keep a list of back-up support and phone numbers ready for quick reference ahead of any emergency.

Cultural influences

Different cultural backgrounds introduce special considerations for some adolescents and families. Fortunately there are multicultural counsellors who can engage with the adolescent (and their parents) in their native language, and have an understanding of cultural nuances.

- As a starting point, try the Multicultural Mental Health Australia website at www.mmha.org.au.
- Also see www.blackdoginstitute.org.au/docs/CALDpaper.pdf.
- Google (accessed from home, or your local library, with a librarian's help if needed) can generate a list of other multicultural mental health references.

4. Getting to assessment
Some ways to overcome teenage reluctance

The myth that puts paid to a young person's hopes of early diagnosis and treatment is simply that children do not experience genuine clinical disorders. 'Childhood is such a happy time,' you see! **Chris**

I would have to say the most important thing I have learnt through my suffering with a mood disorder is this: there are some things you cannot do alone, and getting over depression is one of them. **Sam**

Few young people are keen to be assessed for *anything*—let alone for a mood disorder. Many will resist, either actively or passively—usually denying that there is a problem. Some teenagers are ready to be persuaded by parents or friends if convincing reasons are provided. However, if a teenager can find an excuse for postponing assessment they are likely to grasp it, and sometimes they find implicit support for their resistance from family ambivalence about seeking assessment for a 'mental illness'.

Before considering some of the reasons for avoiding assessment, we offer some concerns about the process as told by teenagers themselves. Their concerns illustrate some of the fears and vulnerabilities that can get in the way. First up, it is hard for a young person to decide that there really is a problem with their feelings that is serious enough to tell someone. Then, if their problem is 'serious enough', they wonder how they will cope with the attendant risks—for some, seeing a counsellor is tantamount to admitting that they are 'mad'. They wonder will they, by admitting their fear and letting down their guard, become even more out of control; will they be forced to take medication, or even be hospitalised?

We have also included some of the writers' suggestions for how to deal with help-avoidance and fears of stigma.

Here is one adolescent's account of his haphazard mastery over a lengthy episode of depression—achieved without systematic help and at some personal cost. It is titled 'Awareness is the Key'.

The thought of seeking professional help outside of the school environment never really occurred to me as it meant involving my parents, something which to this day has been refrained from. With a psychologist mother, help was most probably available, yet this positive aspect was negated by the role my father played—the man's man. To him, any form of weakness, be it physical or mental, was to be frowned upon and, after seeing my two older brothers prevail over the 'trouble years' that are the teens, I was willing to go to extreme measures to prevent being the first child with 'issues'.

So, if and when the adolescent person does decide to seek that professional assistance, the visits are often marred by external circumstances. In my personal experience, upon delving into the entirely unknown world that is school counselling at the ripe yet still innocent age of fourteen, my experience and subsequent attempts at being helped were blocked by the culture prevalent in my high school.

The counsellor, as nice a man as he was, coached the football team I played for in the year preceding the events, and as a result only referred to me by my on-field nickname. On top of this, the 'dark' days continued when, naturally, the children of Year 9 who were experimenting with drugs and alcohol began to take precedence over boys who were suffering recurring depression. Their group status easily overruled the troubles of a fourteen-year-old, and many of my counselling sessions were cancelled or 'postponed' so that the 'cool' groups could spend a lesson in the counsellor's office rather than attend class. Being such a nice man, the college counsellor for my year welcomed them with an open door. Mind you, he and I remained close, exchanging friendly greetings in the hallway, yet this was mainly a result of our sporting exploits rather than any professional relationship developed through my futile attempts to seek help; my socially underdeveloped mind simply accepted this regular occurrence as a fact of secondary school life.

By this stage the 'dark' days were occurring more and more often, yet no attempt was being made to rectify the spiralling situation. One could blame the prevalence of my depression on me the individual, and I do accept some blame for this, yet I see the failure of the counselling system combined with the sporting culture so easily penetrating the attitudes of those within my high school as the largest contributing factor.

Ultimately, informal strategies were put in place by a group of friends that rectified the situations causing my misery, namely, the ever-increasing issue of girls (and the pressure applied by some people around me to have success in this area), and the growing pressures of high school with its '110 per cent' attitude. Being a fourteen-year-old boy, hormones already unpredictably holding my moods captive, these complications provided further reasons to 'over-think' situations and be miserable. This resulted in me turning further inwards.

So, I felt that the people around me could not be trusted, be they classroom teachers, whom the school encouraged you to foster a close personal relationship with, or counsellors, who in this case only saw me as a rugby player, a 'commodity' in a tough team sport, incapable of having serious emotional difficulties or questioning who exactly he was and what his purpose was ... though I did this—more often than not coming up with a blank. Then came my parents, but to let them know of the troubles I was having was to lose face, and in a society based on being a tough and emotionally solid man, this alternative was out of the question, and as a result professional help outside the school environment was crossed off the list of possibilities.

Luckily, most problems solved themselves (by the doings of myself and friends, not professionals) before too much harm was done. Yes, self-harm occurred but on very few occasions, yet it is worth noting these occurred in the months where I was stranded in the limbo between being ignored by counsellors and not being confident enough to talk to friends.

The friends whom I did ultimately confide in were encouraging, upbeat and easy to talk to, characteristics of a friend needed in this situation. Funnily enough, these boys are not my 'best' friends, and we don't socialise outside of school, and rarely in it, yet during those dark periods I relied on them so heavily and it's something I hold them in high esteem for. The strategies they helped me to implement held me in good stead and as a result, three years later, I am happy and enjoying life.

Awareness really is the key, and by encouraging people to foster the treatment of mental health rather than shun it, the state and prevalence of mood disorders and depression in adolescents could be largely rectified, resulting in happier teens. **Jason**

DON'T 'WAIT OUT' A MOOD DISORDER

Individuals with mood disorders—older as well as younger—often decide to wait out the illness rather than seek professional help. Generally, the reasons for hesitation and delay are similar for both parents and adolescents, and stem from uncertainty about what is happening, what might be achieved, and at what cost.

However, where possible, it is important to take action *before* depression becomes established at a level that impairs everyday functioning. As problems increase at school and in the adolescent's relationships (for instance, they might isolate themselves, or take up with individuals or groups that reflect and exacerbate their distress), these are likely to destabilise a teenager even further, as could their adoption of a variety of uncharacteristic behaviours that the teen may come to define as the way they 'really' are if such behaviours are left to develop further.

THE BIG 'D' WORD

In adolescence, depression (the big 'D') can present in such varying ways that it is difficult to be sure whether it is present or not. Its ineffability, combined with reluctance to consider the possibility of a mental illness, and denial that it might be present, means that depression may remain vague—in that it can't be defined in words. It becomes literally 'unspeakable' and is thus not spoken about. As a consequence of stigma, some teenagers and families will actively or passively allow the depression to remain unrecognised, with everyone walking around the elephant in the room, and round and round ...

SOME REASONS WHY ASSESSMENT IS AVOIDED

One major obstacle to seeking assessment is that the adolescent and their carer/s don't recognise what is happening as depression.

> I didn't have the words to say what was happening to me.
>
> In my experience there can be many obstacles to seeking help—denial, fear, the stigma of mental illness, becoming trapped in a routine—but for me the main obstacle was the lack of a 'language' to deal with depression. I was never equipped to deal with depression as a teenager, partly because I didn't know what it was. This is an area where schoolteachers and the school curriculum can play an important role. Perhaps if mental health had been a significant part of the curriculum when I was at school (I don't ever remember discussing mental health issues at school) then instead of thinking of myself as 'unnatural' I might have seen the problem for what it was: a temporary and treatable form of depression that needn't have dominated such an important period of my life to the extent that it did. **Maxine**

> It was not until I was an adult that I was diagnosed with manic depression. I spent my adolescence crippled by the feeling that something was wrong with me and that it didn't have a name. I spent four years waiting to 'snap out of it' and be more like my peers. **Xavier**

There is also the worry that admitting to depression may have worse consequences than waiting for it to abate.

> At the time when my symptoms became noticeable, and over the weeks when I continued not to disclose my real affective and psychotic experiences, my parents engaged in proactive health-seeking behaviours. My parents searched the White Pages, Yellow Pages, internet sites, rang health services looking for an independent means to have my health assessed so that all possible avenues of treatment could be exhausted. During this time, because I was only disclosing physical symptoms, particularly sleep-related issues, my general practitioner was unable to refer me to the appropriate service. I was terrified of being identified as a 'crazy person' because, at the age of twelve I considered such a problem as being a permanent, lifelong condition, a condition which would restrict me from being able to return to mainstream school. I feared I would permanently be considered mentally disabled, I would have problems gaining paid employment, and that if I was identified as a 'crazy person' I may be hospitalised for years at a time, possibly the rest of my life. **Lauren**

There may be no-one to tell, no-one interested enough in the teenager—or they may not be believed. The mood disorder may also be ignored or unnoticed because a person's immediate environment devalues any 'psychological' problems.

> These days I would have been classified by admiring protégés as a 'Metro'! Back then I was called everything from a runt, skinny, bones etc., etc. Not suitable for the environment of a rough, tough mining town. And I soon felt the fact that

my physical stature cast me as an outsider to the other kids! The name-calling began in earnest. I had a close bunch of schoolmates, but even your mates can turn on you when suitable peer pressure is applied.

By age twelve I was spiralling in a closed world of self-doubt and lack of confidence. I had mates at school, got on okay with most, but I was tainted as a kid with little athletic ability and physical strength. The fact that I was considered talented academically simply did not enter into the picture. The ability to play football and cricket was considered far more appealing than an ability to compile a relatively complicated piece of prose! **Sean**

The depression may sometimes be masked by morphing into something different, such as anxiety, an eating disorder, a medical condition or substance abuse.

I developed an addiction to self-loathing. Unable to control or understand the world around me I grew intent on controlling myself. My body was a tangible thing, my progress marked in how small or large my stomach looked at the beginning and end of each day. I rationed myself, and re-rationed until my body adjusted to being underfed. I became regimented, stiff, unloving, prickly in my attitudes towards others, morose and silent. **Rosa**

There may be other problems in the family that focus attention away from the teenager's distress.

My mother was so sick that Dad had enough trouble as it was. I became an expert at masking my depression to the outside world for fear of being labelled an outsider and causing my parents more grief. I once wrote, 'My desolate body still remains on this earth, battered and abused within, yet masked to the world around me.' **Jessie**

Another possibility is that there may be situations of enforced secrecy, such as past or continuing physical and sexual abuse.

OTHER REASONS WHY ASSESSMENT IS AVOIDED

Here are some more reasons offered by teenagers and their families for avoiding assessment. The question is: are they really valid concerns?

'We don't know what's going on and our child can't explain it.'

Many adults lack the words to define or explain distressing experiences; a young person has even less chance. That doesn't mean it isn't happening.

'The mood changes will go away if we leave well enough alone. We don't want to over-react.'

The mood changes may not go away, especially if they've been present for some weeks or more. Even if the teenager's mood improves after a time, anyone who has experienced a serious mood disorder is at risk of a later recurrence.

'Dealing with this—whatever it is—might make it worse.'

Regrettably, there is some truth to this concern. If assessment is undertaken by a practitioner who is insensitive, incompetent and/or provides an incorrect diagnosis and/or inappropriate management, time will be lost and the teen will be reluctant to seek help again. For such reasons, this book aims to provide a template for what should be expected from professional assessment and management.

'My friends will think I'm psycho!'

Worry about the stigma of mental illness shouldn't influence a decision to seek assessment, but rather highlight the need for discretion and sensitivity. How discretion is best managed should be discussed by parents and professionals with the teenager. For example, how is the young person's confidentiality to be handled, and with whom among their friends, family, school counsellors and employers? Such decisions can be made after cautious discussion.

Addressing the label of 'psycho' or other pejorative and stigmatising terms is important. If a teenager is going to tell anyone about being assessed or about a diagnosis, then how should it be presented? For example, some may wish to be very open (and use the actual name of the psychiatric condition); others will prefer a 'medical' euphemism, such as chronic fatigue syndrome or CFS, which has many symptoms in common with depression. The teenager may come up with a plausible alternative explanation for their state, such as 'I'm anaemic', or 'They're running tests on me to find out what's wrong'. While the outcome associated with the least secrecy is the least demanding, some teenagers need time (and good progress) before they can more openly discuss what they are going through.

'Our child will think we're punishing them.'

The situation may be fraught and your child may protest that they are a scapegoat for other (stated or unstated) problems within the family. Indicating your affection, concern and respect may soften a course of action that you recognise is the responsible thing for you, as the parent, to do. There is a power imbalance that can't be disguised.

Using subterfuge to get a teenager to assessment is likely to undermine their trust in you. Telling the young person that they are seeing a doctor for medical reasons and then dropping them at the consulting rooms of a psychiatrist will not work—worse, it is likely to be counterproductive. The teenager will be angry about being deceived and manipulated, will be uncooperative with the psychiatrist, and may then storm around the house (or stay in their room) for days or weeks, and refuse to ever again see a professional.

For those teenagers who are tentatively prepared to accept an assessment, this may be advanced by framing it as being in response to a family problem—with you all needing to find a way to accommodate to each other. The parents might accompany the teen and then ask the professional who should be interviewed first, the adolescent or the parents, or all together.

'I'm scared I may be assessed as mad, or even hospitalised.'

The teenager will be concerned about acknowledging their vulnerability and probably will be worried about whether they are likely to be forced to, for instance, take medication, or even go to hospital. Many will resist assessment by focusing on worst-case scenarios. Here, it is possible to offer a staging model, suggesting that the first stage is merely to get the views of the professional for consideration by all.

'My parents will find out confidential things about me.'

All competent professionals operate to principles that protect confidentiality (unless it is overridden by legal or extreme high-risk situations). For example, a professional might ask the teenager who he/she would like to be interviewed first—the teenager or their parents; or if they would like their parents to sit in on their assessment. Even if the young person turns to their parents for an opinion on that question, the professional should empower them by immediately stating that it is their call. At the beginning of the interview—and later, if the parents subsequently join the interview—the professional should review with the teenager what issues are not for broader discussion at that time, or even at any time.

'I don't want to see someone just yet—there must be information out there.'

Yes, there is a lot of assistance available, ranging from general information, assessment tools and even treatment packages that can be obtained over the internet, allowing the individual to increase their awareness and often to refine diagnostic possibilities.

The Black Dog Institute website (www.blackdoginstitute. org.au) has self-report screening measures for both depression and bipolar disorder. It also offers a Depression Education Program that details our sub-typing model, setting out the types and patterns of depressive disorders, as well as a Bipolar Education Program, which provides diagnostic and management information (including education and a well-being plan).

'We don't know where to go for help.'

At the end of Chapter 3 is a list of some health professionals who provide assessment. Their general training, background and approach to mood disorders are briefly described, but these features are less important than their competence— 'competence' referring as much to the therapist's diagnostic and management model as to their professional and personal characteristics.

In finding a competent professional to provide an assessment, there are wider issues to consider—namely, the diagnostic and treatment models that differing therapists adopt in their daily practice. We now look at these.

DIFFERENT WAYS OF VIEWING DEPRESSION

The dimensional/continuum model

Regrettably, the dominant framework for conceptualising the depressive disorders is a 'dimensional' or 'continuum' model, which views depression as a single condition (an 'it') of lesser or greater severity. This means that practitioners believing in this model tend to offer a single treatment approach to all their clients, along the lines of their own preference—be it antidepressant medication, a psychotherapy or counselling. Basically, the client's depression is 'fitted' to the practitioner's model, training or discipline, rather than treatment being fitted to the individual's actual 'type' of depression (which might need quite differing approaches depending on its origins).

To illustrate the drawback in this approach, consider the following analogy. If you had gone to your doctor because you were struggling for breath, a diagnosis of major or minor 'breathlessness' would not be very informative and certainly not sufficient to shape the treatment and management of your condition. You would expect that the professional you consulted would establish the cause of your breathlessness (e.g. asthma, pneumonia), and then provide a rational treatment (e.g. bronchodilator, antibiotic). Similarly, we hold that the same logic should apply to conceptualising the depressive disorders.

Depression is not a one-size-fits-all 'it'.

All therapies aren't of equal relevance

So, assessment and treatment can be compromised when a professional assumes that depression is a single condition, and then goes on to assume that all therapies are of equivalent relevance to the disorder. The risk of this approach is that some depressive conditions may be overtreated and others undertreated.

As an example of overtreatment, a teenager who has become temporarily depressed as a consequence of a stressor might be encouraged to take antidepressant medication or engage in psychotherapy for an extended period, even long after the stressor and its effects have passed.

Conversely, undertreatment might occur if there was failure to identify a biological depressive illness, such as melancholic or bipolar depression. Medication (alone, or along with education and a wellbeing plan) is usually needed to bring such a condition under control, but the teenager may only be provided with a non-medication treatment approach.

The dangers of a fixed point of view

Another limitation of many therapists is that they have been trained to work within a single framework—be it believing that depression is a 'chemical imbalance' (and therefore always prescribing antidepressants), or that teenage depression must reflect family problems (and therefore always providing family therapy). If the teenager is referred to a therapist who adopts the wrong treatment paradigm, a good outcome is compromised.

Another therapeutic risk is from the therapist who is 'eclectic'. Like a bird building a nest grabbing a piece of blue cotton blowing past, this therapist may listen to the teenager's history and seize upon something that strikes them as worth following—or worse, as *all-explanatory* of the teenager's condition. While such a therapist might be correct on occasions—as one can be when picking the best combination of food from a smorgasbord—the risks are obvious.

These concerns apply for all therapists, but may represent greater risks in assessing and managing mood swings in young people.

The differing speeds of therapists

Therapists may also function at differing speeds. Some take weeks or months to derive a diagnosis and formulation—and some never get to that destination at all. If you ask some clients who have been attending a therapist for years what the therapist's 'game plan' is, many will appear perplexed and note that no plan has ever been mentioned. Such meandering therapy may involve no more than the client reporting on their week.

On the other hand, some therapists work too quickly—are perhaps too brusque, cutting off the individual verbally, or non-verbally (by avoiding eye contact, writing a prescription and bringing the session to an end), or talking over the person.

The 'ideal' therapist

So what should you look for in a psychiatrist or therapist who is to assess a young person? While clearly they need to be able to relate comfortably to the teenager, the therapist's personal style should not take priority over their technical competence. As for all other professional groups there are many personally and professionally 'nice' practitioners who lack some of the key technical skills that are associated with good diagnosis and management.

How do you pick a suitable therapist? Going to a listing, for instance on a website, is problematic. It is easy to advertise but it is hard for those seeking help to assess a therapist's capacity and 'fit' this way. Seeking a recommendation from someone you trust is wise. Perhaps ask your GP, who will have experience of different therapists over time. Or ask others who have walked the same track who they might recommend.

Once you are at the consultation, it is often useful to judge the psychiatrist or therapist on their interpersonal manner and their capacity to provide an explanation that makes sense to you. Judge if their overall formulation of the teenager's problems seems rich rather than narrowed to a simplistic model. Do they appear sensible and engaged and show common sense as you continue to consult them? Importantly, if you have an urgent problem, or if they are absent for a while, you should be able to expect that they will have arrangements in place to handle emergencies and continuity of care for the distressed young person.

. . . .

A FRAMEWORK FOR ACTION

You've observed that a teenager you care for is struggling with some problem that they can't master—probably a mood disorder. Now, how do you get a grasp of the problem so that you can arrange appropriate professional help? And how do you advance a discussion with them without accidentally making things worse? Here are some ways that have been found to be useful in opening up what can be a threatening and painful subject.

First, is an assessment needed?

Hopefully, your gut feeling will tell you whether your teen would benefit from an assessment to see what's going on. An assessment should be discreet and sensitive so that the young person doesn't feel too invaded. Indeed, they won't confide their concerns if they are not comfortable with the counsellor and the setting.

Seek advice for yourself

It may be useful to consult with someone yourself prior to any assessment, in order to get your own thoughts clear. In any case, before you broach the subject with your teenager, it helps to have a basic grasp of what you think might be happening, and an idea of what you want to get out of the discussion.

Books such as this are a good starting point for clarifying what you want to find out, what it might mean, and what you would like to see happen. For example, look over the logical decision-tree diagram at the end of Chapter 2, and the detail provided in Chapter 5 of how an assessment is structured.

Equally important is how you come across to the adolescent in such a discussion. You are the strong and reassuring presence here.

How do you bring up the subject?

You probably know the situations when you and your teen feel most comfortable together. Or you can at least create a time when you can talk together without pressure or interruption, allowing an unhurried discussion. Decide how far you want to press the subject—there is likely to be natural resistance or denial initially, as the young person may be frightened and defensive. If it is too difficult at first, now that you have opened up the subject you could mention a particular time when you will broach it again.

What might you say?

You can let them know what you've noticed and why you are concerned. You are probably their most familiar contact, but it may not make it any easier to raise a sensitive subject that is so close to their sense of themselves, particularly as they are likely to feel that they have lost their bearings. But press on gently.

How do you go about saying it?

There are many books and also guides on the internet about how to talk to a young person about such a delicate topic. They can provide the sort of phrasing and metaphors that might be effective. Generally, such advice covers some simple directives, summed up in the acronym 'sure valley' (SuRe ValLi):

- **Su**pport—offer your warm acceptance and help, without rushing in to swamp the teenager with advice. Try to take things at their pace.
- **Re**spect them and their point of view. Avoid simplistic reassurance.
- **Val**idate what you are hearing, and try not to belittle their problems and distress.
- **Li**sten first. This is crucial. Despite your own anxieties, try not to swamp them with advice and reassurance. And try to suspend value judgments for the present.

What will an assessment achieve?

An assessment will help to decide whether the symptoms are mainly due to depression, another psychological condition or a physical problem. It may result in a diagnosis and a plan of management. Alternatively—to your relief—there may not be a clinical problem at all! In this last instance, the discomfort and worry you felt which led you to seek evaluation may be dissipated by a talk with someone skilled in the area who has seen it all before and who can give you a bit of a road map through the geography of adolescence.

Usually the teenager and parent/s will be interviewed together for part of the time during an assessment. As noted, the counsellor may give the young person the choice of a one-on-one interview first, followed by the parents joining in partway through. Interviews can be separate if requested, though it is important that both the teenager and the care-givers have accurate information about what is happening. The young person should understand that parents can provide useful information about signs and symptoms, including how behaviour is at home and elsewhere and whether it has changed significantly.

Why not just wait it out?

'Waiting out' your teenager's mood disorder is *not* the best option. An untreated depression is not only distressing to the teen and to others, but also distracts from the developmental tasks that they need to negotiate on their way to adulthood. The corrosive effects on self-image can undermine confidence and direction, and for some there is a heightened risk of reckless behaviour.

Depression is also associated with co-occurring conditions (such as anxiety or eating disorders), and patterns of self-harm, including drug and alcohol abuse.

Getting a young person to assessment and then persisting until you have found the right help may be taxing, but such tensions would seem far preferable to the chronic damage that can be sustained if mood disorders are left untreated.

• •

5. Making the diagnosis
Guidelines for a systematic approach

At the time all I wanted was for somebody to listen
to me and to try to understand some of my pain. To
see me, not just glance at me but really see, feel and
understand me. But I often found that I was being placed
into the too-hard basket—ignored because people didn't
understand, and didn't want to. I admit that at times I must
have been extremely challenging, but I was continually
brushed aside. I was taunted by my peers, who called
me a psycho or a freak, and even by adults, including
my high school principal, who told me that I would never
amount to anything and that I'd end up living in a mental
institution. This didn't help my already fragile mental state
but it did make me angry—angry enough to get serious
about wanting to beat my black dog. **Tabitha**

A LOGIC TO THE ASSESSMENT OF MOOD DISORDERS

Professionals—be they GPs, psychologists, social workers, counsellors, psychiatrists or others—all differ in the ways in which
they interview a young person, both in terms of style but, more
distinctly, in terms of the structure and logic that they use.

In this chapter, we overview the sub-typing model that is
employed by our clinicians at the Black Dog Institute. It is a

strong part of the world view embraced by our practitioners in their assessments of both adults and older teens, who are most commonly referred to us by their managing doctor for a second opinion for longstanding and/or unresponsive mood disorders.

Each assessment interview aims to generate a diagnosis as well as a treatment and management plan, which is then formalised in a report sent to the referring doctor. It is important to note that the systematic 'decision tree' outlined in the following pages may not necessarily correspond with the interview structure and style of other psychiatrists.

Please refer to the Glossary and to Appendix IV for explanations of some of the terms used throughout this chapter.

THE CLINICAL INTERVIEW

The clinical interview covers certain set areas. It is designed for adults and older adolescents and systematically works through the many diagnostic and management possibilities. The client completes a computerised Mood Assessment Program (the MAP), which generates information about a range of factors that may be relevant to depression, such as anxiety, mood swings and stressful events. Its diagnostic algorithm then computes the individual's mood state. The MAP is described in Appendix IV.

The clinical interview following on involves a mix of questions, beginning with open-ended ones and leading to more finely focused questions after ten to fifteen minutes. While some practitioners might spend several (and even many) interviews gathering information, we generally allocate an hour to the initial interview and seek by the end of that hour to generate:

- a provisional diagnosis
- a differential diagnosis
- a management plan for discussion with the individual, and
- some information to educate the adolescent and their carers about the mood disorder.

The last few minutes of the interview are then spent discussing any questions raised by the individual (and/or family members).

The model favours a detailed recorded history—with the view that the person appreciates its comprehensive nature—so quite careful notes are written down. However, if they raise a private issue that they would prefer was not put in writing, we may not formally note that detail.

The assessment—initial tasks

The assessment generally starts with a semi-structured question (e.g. 'What can I do to help you?' or 'Could you tell me something about yourself and your problems?'), with the response usually indicating whether the individual is comfortable about the assessment.

If an adolescent begins by speaking openly, then the interviewer can move to a more structured approach. If they appear defensive or guarded, it is important for the interviewer to establish what may lie behind those attitudes. For example, did the teenager feel coerced by a parent to attend an interview—and if so, how can their defensiveness be put at ease? Alternatively, does any diffidence reflect their stress about the interview, and therefore would they be more at ease after some explanation about how the interview is going to proceed?

It is important for the interviewer to state the 'rules' of the interview. For example, the interviewer might say that he/she would be keen to talk with one or both parents after the teenager has been interviewed, but that before doing so they will check whether there are any issues the teenager wishes not to discuss. It is also important to state how widely the interview information will be distributed (e.g. that a summary of the interview will be sent to the referring doctor).

In such scenarios, resistance by the teenager is rare—but this may indicate that those who actually get to the interview have already shown a willingness to talk about the problem, and therefore have overcome the resistance of most teenagers to talking to a professional.

Information about the current mood disorder

An initial priority is to gather information about the current mood disorder and previous depressive and/or manic states— and to note when both have been at their worst.

After asking the young person to describe the key features of such episodes, the interviewer will ask further structured questions that are designed to probe whether the depressions are more likely to be 'melancholic' (quintessentially biological) or 'non-melancholic' in their pattern. There are no explicit symptoms that decisively distinguish between these two broad depressive sub-types. Instead, there are certain features that are more often present in the melancholic sub-type rather than specific to it—a reality that makes this diagnosis more difficult to make. Such melancholic features include:

- distinctive anergia (i.e. lack of energy, not merely fatigue)
- impaired concentration
- slowed and/or agitated movements
- an anhedonic mood state (i.e. the individual gets no pleasure from activities that would normally give pleasure)
- a non-reactive mood (i.e. the individual is either not

cheered up at all by pleasant events, or is only superficially or fleetingly cheered up)

- diurnal variation (i.e. the mood state and the lack of energy are usually worse in the morning and improve later in the day).

Melancholic depression

Melancholic depression, or melancholia, is a very physical, biological state reflecting disrupted neurocircuits in the brain—a sort of chemical imbalance where there is a decrease in neurotransmitter function. This leads to symptoms (features reported by the individual) and signs (features observed by others) of psychomotor disturbance.

The 'psycho' part of 'psychomotor' refers to the impaired concentration experienced during a melancholic episode. Unlike an individual with a non-melancholic depression, who might have a high level of anxiety and so describe impaired concentration as a consequence of anxiety-based distraction, in melancholia the individual is more likely to describe their thoughts as slowed, and that their brain is 'foggy'. One patient stated that he normally cooked for the family at night, but when he was in a melancholic episode, he couldn't even remember the recipe for an omelette. Teenagers with melancholia will generally describe great difficulty in trying to study and an inability to concentrate—even for short periods of time.

The 'motor' part of 'psychomotor' refers to the individual's symptoms of retardation and/or of agitation. Retardation is visible in the melancholic individual: they lose the 'light in their eyes', and feel slowed down physically and mentally. They lack energy (it is a major effort to even get out of bed to have a shower) and feel as if they're walking through molasses or sand.

These two features—impaired concentration and retardation—have led to the description of melancholia as a 'black dog' or a 'black fog'. Many individuals describe an episode commencing with the feeling that they are descending into a 'black hole'.

Motor agitation is another feature of melancholia. This refers to the individual's signs of agitation—maybe a furrowed forehead, slow writhing movements of their hands (and even of their legs), or restless pacing up and down. Many people with motor agitation wake early in the morning with their stomach churning, preoccupied by worries about trivial issues, and unable to settle. Agitation is rarely constant, but more often oscillates with periods of retardation.

As correlates of these changes, the individual with melancholic depression will often become asocial—with no motivation to mix with family or friends, failing to return phone calls or text messages. Their depressed mood is experienced as a sense of blackness, of hopelessness and despair, and feeling that there is no future and that they are worse than worthless.

The interviewer will also be observing the person to see if there are external signs of psychomotor disturbance—although these are only likely to be present if the individual is seen at the worst of the episode. The interviewer will also seek corroborative witness information from a family member who has seen the teenager at their lowest. The interviewer will ask that relative about impaired concentration, retarded and/ or agitated movements, loss of the light in the eyes, diurnal variation, and reduced reactivity to pleasant and normally mood-cheering events.

Psychotic depression

If a diagnosis of melancholic depression is made, the interviewer will then clarify whether or not the teenager has experienced a psychotic sub-type of melancholia. If psychosis is present, the individual is likely to have shown symptoms and signs of an even more distinct level of psychomotor disturbance, but a diagnosis of psychotic depression also requires the presence of categorical psychotic features: delusions and/or hallucinations.

Such psychotic features may be 'mood congruent', where the individual describes delusional preoccupations or auditory hallucinations that mirror the despair and severity of their depressed state. For example, they may be convinced that they deserve to be dead or severely punished; or they may describe a voice saying that they are 'worthless' or accusing them of some other negative attribute, with the voice usually quite distinct (rather than vague and indecipherable, as occurs more commonly in schizophrenia). Or they may be certain that the depression is a deserved punishment, and cannot be convinced that their delusional beliefs are false. ('Mood incongruent' delusions, e.g. that the person is possessed by aliens, can also be experienced by those with a psychotic depression and do not necessarily indicate schizophrenia.)

The possibility of a psychotic depression should be closely investigated in those who show a severe melancholic depression marked by guilt—and the nature of the guilt should be clarified to see whether the individual holds it at a delusional level or not. For example, the adolescent who acknowledges that they feel guilty and that they deserve to be punished for some minor indiscretion from the past may well be showing such psychotic guilt. By contrast, the adolescent who feels guilty merely because they are letting their parents down is more experiencing the 'normal guilt' that is felt by most people with a disabling depressed state—it does not, at that level, equate to delusional or overvalued ideas of guilt.

Bipolar or unipolar course
The interviewer will then look for any evidence of another biological type of mood state—that is, whether the individual

has had a bipolar illness course, or a unipolar one. (In unipolar depression, there are swings from normal mood into depression, but no highs.)

A bipolar disorder is shown by oscillations in mood and energy. In contrast to the melancholic state, where energy and mood levels are extremely low, during a high the individual will describe the converse: elevations of mood and energy. In terms of mood, they will feel carefree, extremely happy and overconfident. In terms of energy, they will describe feeling highly energised and wired, full of plans and capable of achieving virtually anything. On questioning, they are likely to say that they need less sleep and don't feel tired, and admit to exaggerated behaviours such as being verbally indiscreet (e.g. saying overly frank things that they wouldn't normally say), or impulsive and incautious behaviour (e.g. having tattoos done that are later regretted, or being sexually promiscuous). Normal anxieties disappear and the individual feels carefree and euphoric, although some will describe intertwined levels of irritability and anger. They will often spend lots of money purchasing goods such as clothes, CDs and other attractors, and adults are at risk of significant financial misadventures.

Bipolar sub-type

The interviewer will then seek to establish any bipolar sub-type. In a Bipolar I disorder, the individual will have experienced psychotic features—becoming out of touch with reality in their highs. In Bipolar II, psychotic features are not experienced during the highs and rarely, if at all, during any melancholic depressive episode.

If a bipolar picture is suggested, the interviewer will try to determine whether any such highs have occurred spon-taneously. If they have only come on after the person has taken antidepressant medication, or after an increase in its dose or following its cessation, this condition is known as Bipolar III, and is medication-induced rather than a true bipolar state. If it is only associated with illicit stimulant drug use, a bipolar disorder may still be present (i.e. highs may be driving the taking of drugs), but is less likely.

Risk assessment

At some stage of the interview—probably after reviewing clinical symptoms—an assessment of suicide risk must be made for any teenager with a mood disorder. A direct question such as 'Are you having any suicidal thoughts?' is appropriate, and likely to be expected by the young person. If the answer is yes, the interviewer will enquire into any plans or attempts, and any related self-injurious behaviours, and then make some judgment about risk. The interviewer will maintain the same tone of voice in the interview as when asking questions of less concern. More detail about risk assessment is provided in Appendix II.

Stressful events

Either before or after gathering information about the mood disorder, the interviewer will ask about stressful events that preceded the episode/s (whether 'always', 'usually', 'rarely' or 'never'). This is both to obtain a general picture and to determine if depressive episodes are effectively explained by such stressors.

While melancholic depression is less likely to be associated with stressors (it was previously called 'endogenous depression' to reflect that it came 'from within'), it can't be assumed that the absence or presence of stressors is a clue to whether the depression is melancholic (unipolar or bipolar) or non-melancholic—especially in the case of adolescents. While a history of stressors is not particularly discriminating as to the type of depression, if an adolescent states that their depressive episodes happen without any obvious stressor, then this weights the likelihood of the disorder being of the melancholic sub-type.

Other information about the disorder

Age of onset
The interviewer will then move on to establish the age of onset of depressive (and any bipolar) episodes. Melancholic depression and bipolar disorder are very rare in childhood, and generally emerge in adolescence at the earliest.

Past treatments
Next, the interviewer will list all treatments received by the individual and evaluate their cost–benefit. Here, the interviewer is looking to see what past treatments, if any, have been effective, to what degree, and whether there have been significant side-effects that have limited the value of these effective treatments.

Developmental history
The interview will then move on to a developmental history. This has several objectives. First, it aims to get a snapshot of how the adolescent has progressed through life until now and to better know and understand them. Second, it is designed to see if there is any corroborative support for a biological melancholic depression and, if there is not, to determine what factors might have contributed to a non-melancholic depression.

Thus, the interviewer will ask about the family—finding out who constitutes the family circle, whether there is any family history of a mood disorder (this might support a more 'biological' mood state), and the quality of the adolescent's parenting. Low levels of parental care, and indifference and abuse—as well as parental overprotection—may have set the stage for later non-melancholic depressive episodes.

The **ordinal position** of the teenager within the family will be noted (i.e. only child, eldest child, youngest child) as this can shape personality style. Some assessment of the individual's **early temperament** style (e.g. shy, loner, sociable) will be sought from the teenager as well as from the parents' observations (with the parents also being asked whether there were any **birth complications** or early significant **illnesses**).

Next, the interviewer will ask about the ability over time of the adolescent to read books and to **concentrate** in class for their primary school years. This is to exclude the possibility of an attention deficit hyperactivity disorder (ADHD), which can sometimes falsely suggest a diagnosis of early-onset bipolar disorder. The interviewer will also look for evidence of **early personality problems**, as manifested in conduct problems in the classroom and by conflict with peers.

The interviewer will also delicately follow up whether there were any issues of **abuse** (bullying or verbal, physical or sexual abuse) and gently enquire about these in order to judge how severe they were, their salience and their capacity for ongoing effects.

Progress through secondary school (in terms of academic progress, peer relationships, socialisation and any bullying experiences) is also investigated. If the adolescent has left school, their work choices and work history will also be explored.

Next, the nature of **close relationships** is sensitively explored, keeping in mind that many teenagers may feel ashamed that they have never had a close or intimate relationship, while others may be preoccupied by a perceived failure in relationships, and others may have concerns about their sexual or gender identity.

The interviewer will move on to information about any relevant **medical condition** or **history of allergies**—particularly as some individuals with a food intolerance history will show drug intolerance reactions to medication.

The presence of any **lifetime anxiety disorder** (such as generalised anxiety, panic disorder, agoraphobia, social phobia, obsessive compulsive disorder) will be assessed by systematic probe questions and, if affirmed, by follow-up questions to establish the likelihood of the teenager meeting diagnostic criteria for any of those anxiety disorders.

Drug and alcohol use

A drug and alcohol history will next be explored, with the drug history ranging from details about illicit drugs, through to intake of caffeine and high-energy drinks, which can contribute to high levels of anxiety in depressed adolescents.

Personality style

The interviewer will then move on to make some assessment of the adolescent's personality style, to establish the relevance of the following traits. Are they: an anxious worrier (or do they externalise any anxiety with irritability); overly sensitive to interpersonal interactions; socially introverted; reserved in interpersonal relationships; impulsive and with a hair-trigger emotional response to provocation; and/or perfectionistic?

Research by the Institute shows that certain personality styles predispose individuals to develop mood disorders (particularly non-melancholic depression) following stressful events that have special significance for them because of previous exposure to similar stressors (such as abuse or criticism). To use an analogy, this predisposition is like a lock and key where, for instance, what looks to others like an exaggerated response to a particular stressor may make perfect sense when one understands the individual's background and unique vulnerabilities. In consequence, the personality style can shape the clinical pattern. (See also the section on personality styles in Chapter 7.)

Referral information

The interview process may or may not be assisted by the following referral information: an interview with parents and other family members; information from the adolescent's school; and contact with any previous treating professional, ideally with their reports being obtained. Such enquiries (whether at the time of the interview or at a later stage) are made with the permission of the young person.

Involvement of family members

At the end of the interview, the interviewer will ask the teenager's permission to have family members sit in at the next stage. As noted earlier, the interviewer will invite the teen to declare issues that they do not want raised with their family. During this family interview, the interviewer will clarify issues that remain unclear, and then discuss the likely diagnosis and management options.

The logic of formulating a diagnosis

The interviewer will then seek to make a diagnosis. There may be a biological mood disorder (i.e. psychotic depression, melancholic depression, bipolar disorder), or a non-melancholic mood disorder.

If it is a non-melancholic disorder, the interviewer will formulate likely contributing factors. Non-melancholic depression may reflect proximal (recent) and precipitating stresses—such as depression coming on after a recent breakup in a relationship—or distal (past) stresses—such as uncaring parents, childhood sexual abuse—and/or a personality contribution (where the personality styles noted earlier can increase the risk of the adolescent developing depression) and/or other contributing factors (for example, drug or alcohol abuse).

Issues of confidentiality

The interviewer should outline the limits of confidentiality with all involved present. The teenager should understand that there are circumstances under which confidentiality will be waived, such as if the interviewer determines that the young person is a risk to themselves and/or others and/or if there is legal involvement.

The extent to which matters are discussed openly, semi-openly or guardedly depends on the wishes stated by the teenager before the family is brought into the interview, and on other key factors such as the maturity of the adolescent, the degree to which the family is unified or divisive, and whether identified issues might be used against the teen by their family. However, the more open the discussion, the better.

There are several aims of this group discussion. Psychiatrists once used to rank the individual's confidentiality above all other issues—admirable on the face of it, but with some difficult and limiting consequences. In such circumstances, families feel locked out and, being left unaware of the teenager's diagnosis and the contributing factors, may respond in inappropriate ways. So, as the young person is usually part of a family, management ideally involves 'buy in' by all relevant family members. Secondly, irrespective of the maturity of the young person, he or she is likely to be somewhat overwhelmed by the interview process, and is thus likely to benefit from a family member acting as a witness. The witness can note the diagnosis, suggested management options, technical particulars (for instance, any antidepressant medication treatment and its dose), and associated details.

The ongoing value of a detailed formulation

If the interviewer has identified a biological (melancholic or psychotic) depression, then many of the other details obtained in the interview will provide background knowledge for more work with the teenager—be it as simple as knowing what school they go to, what year they are in, and whether or not they are in a relationship.

For those with a non-melancholic disorder, the interviewer will be working out the principal drivers of the depression to address a number of the social and psychological factors that have been identified. For example, the adolescent may be depressed because of the severity of the identified stressors and/or by their impact, which might have been accentuated by, for example, longstanding anxiety, which in turn may be inflated by personality style. (Personality styles are further explored in Chapter 7.)

A MANAGEMENT APPROACH DERIVED FROM THE FORMULATION

For each of the differing depressive disorder types and broad patterns, our approach is a 'horses for courses' management model. Thus, for some biological mood disorders experienced by teenagers, the priority will be the prescription and monitoring of medication. For other disorders, medication may be considered as aiding improvement, but not as the mainstay of treatment. Yet again, for other disorders, non-medication options (such as counselling, problem solving, psychotherapy, anxiety management strategies) will be the management tools. Thus, the treatment approach will be shaped by the formulation derived from the interview. The management plan will not select a treatment option merely because it has some longstanding or immediate appeal.

The logic behind the management plan

The logic of the management plan is to work out why this particular adolescent is depressed at this particular time, and for what individual reasons. Specifically, the aim is to decide what factor/s seem to be driving the depression which, if these factors are neutralised or corrected, would improve or abort the depressive syndrome.

. . . .

A FRAMEWORK FOR ACTION

An assessment by a mental health professional must be carried out with empathy and understanding and should allow the young person enough time to express their thoughts and feelings. It is a good idea to check what level of confidentiality will apply to the topics discussed. Decide who will be present at the interview. A teenager can give informed consent from the age of fifteen, but those younger than this need parental consent to seek psychological services for themselves.

Following is a simple summary of the model we use for assessing, diagnosing and managing mood disorders in young people.

The Black Dog Institute approach

Our assessment model uses a systematic decision tree to provide:

- a provisional diagnosis
- a differential diagnosis
- a management plan
- information about the mood disorder for the adolescent and their carers.

At the start of the assessment, the interviewer:

- begins with open-ended questions to assess the teenager's level of comfort with the process, to settle them and to hear about what has been happening in the adolescent's own words
- outlines the 'rules' of the interview—what will be covered, what's on and off the record, how widely the information will be circulated and the circumstances of confidentiality
- focuses in on the current disorder and any previous strategies used to manage it.

As the interview progresses, the interviewer:

- assesses whether the disorder is likely to be:
  - melancholic or non-melancholic depression
  - psychotic depression
  - a bipolar or unipolar disorder
  - if bipolar, what sub-type
- assesses the likelihood of risk (to self, others)
- examines stressful events and their likely impact
- looks at the age of onset and any past treatments and response

- considers the teen's developmental history:
    - family history and background
    - illnesses, injuries, disabilities
    - personality and any personality problems
    - progress through school
    - relationships
    - any history of allergies
    - evidence of any other disorder
- drug and alcohol use
- personality style.

At the close of the interview, the interviewer:

- clarifies the involvement of family members
- formulates the diagnosis and discusses it with the teen-ager and carers
- outlines a management approach.

. . . .

6. The assessment report
And how teenagers adjust to the diagnosis

Finally a diagnosis of bipolar disorder was given
by a psychiatrist who wouldn't give up. He sought
other opinions from other eminent psychiatrists and a
consensus was reached. Finally, David was given the right
medication, a cocktail of antidepressants, antipsychotics
and lithium. I began to see glimmers of my former son. He
started to tell jokes again—laugh—love—live. **Liza**

At the Black Dog Institute (and as is the practice of other
professionals, too), once our clinicians have completed their
assessment of a person's mood disorder (through the systematic
process detailed in Chapter 5), their findings are summarised
in a report that is sent back to the referring health practitioner.
This report covers the adolescent's difficulties and likely
diagnosis, and will also act as a record for the initial management plan.

While this material may be a bit technical and 'medical'
for some readers, we felt that many parents and carers would
appreciate a sense of the sort of information that might be
considered relevant to a management plan for an adolescent
with depression.

Two examples are now provided.

A REPORT TO THE TEEN'S GP

Here is a sample report written to the referring GP, in which the adolescent is referred to a psychiatrist for assessment and ongoing management.

Dear Doctor A,

Thank you for referring Steven Evans, aged sixteen. He described a number of problems at interview. In terms of depression, he related episodes from the age of ten (when he was being heavily bullied, with such episodes tending to last weeks or months). His current episode commenced about four months ago, with features suggestive of a melancholic depression—in that he feels slowed down, his concentration is impaired and he has an anhedonic and anergic mood. He did acknowledge suicidal ideation but denied any plans.

In terms of treatment, he does not feel that his current antidepressant (fluoxetine, 10–40 mg over the last two months) has helped, although his mother believes that there has been some improvement while he has been on this medication.

I wondered about a possible Bipolar II disorder as he does describe times when his mood is elevated and he becomes noisy and disinhibited, full of energy, verbally indiscreet, needs less sleep, spends considerable amounts of money and gambles excessively. However, as such episodes only occur when he has been drinking, it is unclear whether they reflect the impact of intoxication or a sub-clinical Bipolar II disorder being activated by alcohol. This possible diagnosis will need to be clarified.

The diagnosis of a melancholic depression is supported by a very strong family history of mood disorders and with two relatives having taken their life as a consequence.

I note that Steven had been diagnosed with dyslexia in primary school—with further investigations supportive of that diagnosis three years ago. However, this has been of less import in the last two years and is not clearly compromising his current academic performance.

He is socially shy and personally reserved, with noticeable problems in socialising. No relationship with a girl has lasted beyond two weeks and he is painfully aware that they are responding to his seeming indifference to them—which he correctly views as reflecting his shyness. He is, however, able to maintain relationships with some of his male friends, except when in severe depressive episodes.

He is a worrier, and unassertive, and meets criteria (since early childhood) for social phobia. While he has some obsessional symptoms (i.e. counting steps while walking) he does not meet criteria for obsessive compulsive disorder, either in terms of severity and impairment.

I felt that we should prioritise treating his mood disorder initially and, to that end, we agreed that he might taper the fluoxetine and trial a broader-action antidepressant (venlafaxine, 75–150 mg). He has been advised about the problems associated with his alcohol intake (which I interpret as reflecting his attempt to de-stress and to override his shyness), and he believes he can manage that himself. Once his mood disorder has been brought under control, I will refer him to a psychologist to address his unassertiveness and shyness problems, and consider whether any other strategies will need to be put into place.

In this example, Steven's assessment has identified the likelihood of a 'biological' melancholic depressive disorder

100 / **NAVIGATING TEENAGE DEPRESSION**

as the main concern for initial management, and prioritised antidepressant medication to bring it under control, with an initial medication change that will require review after two to three weeks.

Though Steven has suggestions of highs, the initial interview established that these only occurred when he was drinking alcohol, which could suggest either a primary mood elevation from alcohol, or that the alcohol suppressed his shyness and social anxiety and promoted disinhibited (lacking self-control) behaviours. Nevertheless, the potential for alcohol to become an independent problem has been noted, and alcohol use will need to be monitored and a program initiated if Steven is unable to bring his drinking under control himself.

Steven has had distinctive developmental limitations due to his social anxiety, shyness and unassertive personality style—and these may have been increased by his dyslexia; such personality traits are also compromising his current socialisation and quality of life, and may, in themselves, be adding another layer of 'depression'. These problems need to be addressed, but it has been judged that it would be wiser to focus first on treating his melancholic depression, as his response to a psychologist-based intervention is likely to be better when his mood disorder is under more control.

Thus, the assessment interview has identified high-priority problems for immediate management, as well as longstanding problems that will require a quite different paradigm for later management.

While those two problem areas are at one level independent, there are almost certainly interdependencies (e.g. bullying and shyness contributing to depression and Steven's inability to maintain relationships; and his depression leading to asocial, unassertive and shy behaviours).

A REFERRAL TO A PSYCHIATRIST

In the next scenario, Barbara is referred to a psychiatrist by a GP who is willing to provide ongoing management, and who seeks diagnostic clarification (having judged already that the teenager has had a biological depression) to shape the management plan.

Dear Dr B,
Re Ms Barbara Brown, aged sixteen
Thank you for referring this young girl who has recently returned to live with her mother, stepfather and stepsister, and who has been estranged from her father in recent years. She is currently on Youth Allowance and attending TAFE three days a week, preparing for the HSC. We note the assessment by a previous psychiatrist in your referral in regard to depression.

On assessment today, Barbara stated she had been depressed for eighteen months, and that this has occurred in the context of family conflict, particularly with her stepfather and stepsister. In those interactions, she feels both a need to defend her mother and that she is rejected from that family unit. She has had a number of recent stressors including breaking up with a boyfriend, the loss of her job and a serious illness in her grandmother, with whom she is close.

She reports that her mood is sad and angry, and that she feels life, at times, is futile. She sleeps twelve hours per night, reports a loss of appetite and lacks motivation to study. Her concentration is impaired, as she feels quite worried and distracted. She denied any significant guilt. She reports her mood as being able to be lifted at times by pleasant events. She continues to enjoy seeing her friends and her mood also improves with the use of marijuana, which she states allows her to relax.

She admits to suicidal ideation, intermittently over the last three years, but is unclear of the frequency or duration of these states. She has had thoughts of taking an overdose of drugs, but says she tries to calm down and has not taken any action on these thoughts, which are often precipitated by family conflict. She does have a history of deliberate self-harm, cutting, scratching and hitting her legs, beginning when she was twelve. She has cut about five times, usually when angry, but also when low in mood. This usually follows criticism by someone close to her and is a means of punishing herself. She states she experiences some relief following cutting and she last cut about three weeks ago. She has some fantasies of revenge but has not acted on these thoughts and has no current plan to do so.

She also reports irritability, of at least two years' duration, which may last up to hours. This, however, is not associated with any increased energy, racing thoughts, increased creativity, spending, confidence or disinhibition, and she does not regret her actions. Thus, the pattern is not consistent with a hypomanic diagnosis—nor are there any other features to support that possibility.

She commenced escitalopram in January 2008 and is now on 10 mg mane [in the morning], with possible akathisia as an initial side-effect. However, she has noted some benefit to her mood, particularly regarding her irritability. She has seen several counsellors in recent times without clear benefit, but did report that a period of counselling following her parents' divorce had been helpful.

She admits to a history of anxious worrying—particularly in the last year—regarding the unpredictability of relationships, and she has been more sensitive to rejection and criticism. She has some obsessional features, such as relating to even numbers and retracing her writing, which has caused some slowness, but she denies that this is significantly time consuming or distressing at its current level of severity.

She has no significant medical history.

Her current medication is escitalopram 10 mg mane. She is on the oral contraceptive pill. She has no known allergies. She smokes 20 cigarettes per day and uses up to six standard drinks/day, once per month. She began using marijuana at thirteen and has used it daily for the last six months, currently taking 20 cones/day, but previously up to 35. She has also used stimulants—including speed, ecstasy and cocaine—intermittently, and last six months ago. There is no intravenous drug-use history.

She has a paternal aunt who has apparently been diagnosed with schizophrenia and her father has been diagnosed as having a bipolar disorder.

Her developmental history is characterised by the experience of conflict in the parental marriage leading to their divorce. She then had intermittent contact with her father, and although she felt cared for by both parents for a period, is no longer in contact with her father due to his anger at her drug taking. Her mother has been in a relationship for the last three years and she describes ongoing conflict with her stepfather and stepsister and that she feels cut off from this family unit. She began to rebel in late primary school, engaging in truancy and running away from home in her early teens. However she has no history of conduct disorder. Of importance, she reports a number of situations of sexual abuse, including within a previous relationship, beginning at thirteen, and which she states she has 'blocked out' and has only recently revealed to some people. She has maintained some long-term friendships in the past, but these have not continued and she has felt let down by a number of trusted people. She admits to longstanding poor self-esteem, however she has some plans for the future, including hopes of recruitment into the Army.

On mental status examination today she was casually dressed, with a number of piercings and tattoos. She was restless, picking at her nails, and tearful at times, but she could smile briefly and fully, particularly as the interview progressed. Her speech was normal, although initially a little reluctant. She described her mood as about 60 per cent and her affect was sad and dysphoric but—as noted—quite reactive. She denied any current risk to herself and she has no current intention or plan to harm others. She has some insight into her condition and is motivated towards treatment.

On collateral history from her parents, difficulties with low mood and angry outbursts were identified, but there were no observed periods of elevated mood.

While a definite diagnosis cannot be given, we suspect two main possibilities. The first—based on assessment today—is that the current presentation can be explained by issues within her development related to disruption and insecurities in the family structure, and to a number of events that occurred in adolescence that were particularly traumatic, leading to poor self-esteem and hypervigilance, irritability and high anxiety levels.

The other possibility is that of a biological depression, especially given the family history, but this was not supported on our historical review.

We have discussed this diagnosis with Barbara and, with

her permission, her mother. We have suggested that the key priority is to refer her to a psychologist for (a) counselling that will work through the abuse and family conflict issues, (b) a cognitive behavioural program addressing her low self-esteem and other contributing personality issues, and (c) provision of an anxiety reduction program. If successful, we would doubt whether her current antidepressant needs to be continued. If a clear biological depression evolved, we would suggest considering a trial of a broader-acting, dual-action antidepressant, although she would need to be closely monitored for the development of any side-effects, such as agitation, especially given the experience of some akathisia on escitalopram.

It would be important to consider whether her marijuana use has become an independent problem needing attention or whether her use settles when her mood problems are brought under control.

We will be happy to review the outcome of these strategies as required.

In this example, while the referring GP believes that Barbara has a biological type of depression—particularly noting the strong genetic history—this report indicates that the assessing psychiatrist felt Barbara was likely to be experiencing a non-melancholic depression. This is because Barbara did not have a symptom pattern consistent with a melancholic depression (or even a bipolar disorder). Also, she had experienced a number of stressors over an extended period that would have impacted on her self-esteem and security, leading to both depression and anxiety, and to a number of 'acting out' distress behaviours (drug use, self-injury) and stress-reducing behaviours (she viewed the marijuana as settling her anxiety).

If this formulation was correct, and Barbara was sufficiently motivated to take up the strategies and program that would be delivered by a psychologist, then some improvement in self-image, anxiety, depression (and possible drug use) would be anticipated.

It would then be appropriate to taper and cease the antidepressant, which might initially have been of benefit in settling her anxious worrying—and to some degree, her depression—but is likely to be of diminishing relevance after successful non-medication therapy.

THE IMPACT OF THE DIAGNOSIS

> ... being diagnosed with a mental illness I just found such a shock it floored me, literally floored me. For about two weeks I wandered around in a daze at night time, grieving ... I know what grief feels like in losing somebody that you love and I felt that grief—that I'd lost 'me'. **FJ, Bipolar Disorder Education Program, Black Dog Institute**

What is the effect, now that the teen's assessment is completed and it has been judged that there is a mood disorder that requires vigilance and management?

Many who are assessed will receive a diagnosis. For some, this is a relief, because what is 'known' is able to be managed, but for others, being diagnosed with a mental illness such as bipolar disorder or depression will be confronting.

However, this knowledge gives many individuals some immediate (or delayed) power over the disorder: being given a name for what feels wrong confers the capacity to manage it. When it is known that there is a biological or 'hard-wiring' problem, this can also take away the self-blame that some feel.

And it is also validating—they now know they are not just imagining or exaggerating their symptoms.

A missed diagnosis, however, can be very damaging. This is when a serious mental health issue is *not* detected. There is currently, for instance, inadequate detection of bipolar disorder. Sometimes, a depressive episode may be part of a bipolar disorder, and if the individual is treated for depression only—rather than for bipolar—this can lead to treatment complications. Or a skilled assessment may uncover periods of elevated mood, but this may be mistakenly diagnosed as a bipolar disorder when it is more a reaction to the antidepressant drug. The actual diagnosis of bipolar disorder may take up to fifteen years from onset,[1] resulting in distress and unnecessary disruption to the individual's life.

Being given a diagnosis is not so easy for a teenager. For those with a biological condition, there is the impact of having some 'mechanical' problem that may compromise their life trajectory—particularly in terms of their relationships and careers. For others, there is still the issue of stigma.

Here are some accounts that capture teenagers' concerns—and some of their responses and advice.

> … about two weeks after I had got over the shock of my diagnosis [Bipolar I] I thought, 'Well, what am I going to do?' I have to actually work out what this is, what this illness is. If I had some other illness, if I had diabetes or cancer or whatever, I would want to know everything about it so that I could manage it as best as I could, so that I could have control over me and the illness and so that I had the most chance of controlling it instead of it controlling me.
>
> So, we sought a lot of information and it started to make a big difference in my attitude, because that was when we

learnt that it's a chemical imbalance in the brain and that's what mental illnesses are. They are physical illnesses, they're a chemical imbalance in the brain and that's a physical illness just like, if you have diabetes you don't produce enough insulin, that's a chemical imbalance and I have bipolar and I have a chemical imbalance in my brain and I shouldn't feel stigmatised, I shouldn't stigmatise myself, and I shouldn't feel stigmatised by other people because I have a chemical imbalance.

So, we started to have acceptance of that, of it being a physical illness that manifests itself psychologically and that took away a lot of the pain and grief that I was feeling and it gave me acceptance, gradual acceptance of it. **FJ, Bipolar Disorder Education Program, Black Dog Institute**

At that stage, I knew that perhaps the malicious mind monologue of self-pity and self-hatred wasn't normal, but what exactly was wrong with me?

I broke down crying during a doctor's consultation, when she figured out that the reason why I wasn't eating was because I hated myself, and I hated myself because I had a mood disorder called 'social phobia'. This is a variant of depression that explained the years of why I curled up in a dark corner with a book whenever my parents dragged me along to dinner parties. Why I dreaded school assemblies in case I won an award and had to go up on the stage. Why I had panic attacks whenever I thought of the future and what was expected of me in a world that answered phones and knocked on doors. As the doctor handed me a pamphlet about social phobia, the bullet points on the glossy paper read like a script from my life. But I had to be in that room, salted eyes and frail with exhaustion, to hear those words and have them mean something to me. And to know what to do.

A doctor's scribblings in a manila folder makes the situation real, but then what? I went home with my pamphlet and a video to show Mum. We watched it together and cried. She was relieved that I finally accepted that something was 'wrong' with me. Now it was time for action. I went on antidepressants and saw a counsellor twice a week. I was given therapy tasks to get me out into the world; small steps, like saying hello to my uni classmates, instead of blushing or muttering my way through tutorials.

After two years of medication, a regular exercise routine and counselling, I had my first job, was invited to parties and even had the courage to ask someone on a date. Thus, I managed to reach some semblance of normality. But I am an actor in the farce that is the 'normal' world. I find I lapse into negative self-talk if I go even a day without physical exercise, or am not challenged mentally at work. **Nathan**

My big problem as an adolescent [with bipolar disorder] was, first and foremost, embarrassment. As a close second came loss of reputation. Then the rebuilding of a particularly fragile personality after my diagnosis. I hadn't meant to but I'd antagonised my whole family, alienated the few friends I had and made a laughing stock of myself. This is what I've never been able to handle: the stupidity of this condition! My older brother, who also suffers bipolar, is extremely understanding. When I apologised after nearly ruining his career while in a manic state, he said, 'You've just been manic and you did manic things. Everyone who loves you understands.' Who could ask for more than this?

When I was manic I'd turn into the most self-absorbed egotistic loudmouth show-off. I am by nature very shy and easily embarrassed. It certainly has taught me a bit of tolerance for human behaviour. For years I hated being labelled with this mental illness, saw it as a character flaw, a genetic deviancy, and was very, very rough on myself and despised 'me'. I couldn't even stand other people with it either. They were like me, I thought disparagingly, weak, selfish and crazy people. Like me. WRONG! **Troy**

Remember, if you have been diagnosed with a mood disorder, although at first this news may seem like a lonely and frightening journey that you have ahead of you, you are not alone. Surround yourself with family members and friends who lift you up, not drag you down.

Aim to eat well and healthily. Get regular rest, take your required medication that has been prescribed to you and try to fit in some regular exercise, set goals and work towards achieving them. Steer clear of alcohol and recreational drugs. Make time to focus on a hobby in your spare time, something you enjoy that makes you feel happy and good about yourself. For me, this hobby is theatre in the areas of acting, directing and watching plays. This makes me feel inspired and motivated; for you this hobby may be a particular sport, singing, dancing, painting, drawing, or writing stories or poetry.

Most importantly don't let a mood disorder hold you back from following your dreams and living a happy and fulfilled life. Taking the first step and asking for help, although very worrying and daunting at first, is a very small step to take in comparison to letting the years of your life pass by—going through the motions of living, but not really enjoying life to the full. **Poppy**

So, as we have seen, teenagers can have many different initial reactions to diagnosis:

- a blank—the diagnosis may come as a shock, and the implications are only processed slowly
- relief—*So there is something going on, it's not just my imagination*
- concerns about the impact on career and relationships—*What will this mean for my future?*
- fear of stigma—*I'm not psycho!*
- denial—*There's nothing wrong with me*
- *I'm not taking that stuff*—prescription of medication brings with it a range of attitudes. Few people are happy taking medication on an ongoing basis, and adolescents likely to be even less so.

• •

A FRAMEWORK FOR ACTION

A skilled counsellor can make a big difference at the time of diagnosis, and into the future. If you are not comfortable with the health professional that you consult initially, persist in seeking out someone in whom you feel confidence.

The benefits of a counsellor

A counsellor can:

- reassure, familiarise, and pick out and deal with the behavioural, social, emotional and educational aspects of the mood disorder side-by-side with the young person
- help to negotiate any gaps between paediatric and adult services, advise parents and, if needed, inform teachers
- help parents/carers understand how psychiatric services operate, and also provide information about support groups

- act as someone who is 'there' for the young person, and at one remove from the disorder—which means they may be able to encourage and accompany the adolescent on a quest to educate themselves to gain control over the disorder
- define and confine the place of the disorder in the teen's life and work with them, over time, to draw up a wellbeing plan that is tailored to their needs and lifestyle.

Chapter 8 lists ideas for how to build a wellbeing plan.

• •

7. A quick look at treatment and management
And the impact of personality style

Official guides say that to be classified as a sufferer of depression you have to be feeling a number of things for a period of a few weeks. But in truth, it's much more than that.

I was diagnosed with clinical depression when I was in Year 9. I've never really spoken about my experiences openly before and even find it difficult to communicate with my parents sometimes. But let me tell you this: depression affects more than just your mood. I may not know too many facts and statistics about depression, but I do know that I would not have come as far as I have come now without the help of my family, friends and the various doctors I have consulted. **Sam**

In this chapter, we will look at the idea that different types of mood disorders benefit from differing approaches—as they have differing causes. Our Institute publications for professionals have considered treatment approaches in some detail—for both the depressive (Parker and Manicavasagar 2005)[1] and bipolar conditions (Parker 2008)[2]—so we will provide only a brief overview here.

DEPRESSION

We suggest that there are three basic types of clinical depression:

- melancholic depression
- psychotic depression
- multiple expressions of non-melancholic depression.

Each type (as detailed in earlier chapters) has different internal and external causes, arguing for differing treatment approaches. Here we will look at **melancholic** and **psychotic** depression, and patterns of **non-melancholic** depression—turning to a consideration of bipolar disorder later in the chapter.

Melancholic depression

Melancholic depression has a strong genetic and biological loading. Episodes of depression can start without any external stressors. For those episodes following a triggering situation or event, the depressive response is much greater than the trigger seems to warrant. This is a clue that the true cause of the depression is biological. The biological changes impact on brain chemistry, shaping the very physical symptoms of melancholic depression (as mentioned earlier).

In melancholic depression, the treatment priority is to address the root physical process caused by the disrupted flow of chemicals in the brain. In other words, the priority for a physical cause is a physical treatment. This usually involves starting antidepressant medication. However, not all antidepressants are equally effective for melancholic depression.

Classes of antidepressants
Put simply, antidepressants fall into three classes: narrow-action, dual-action and broad-action medications. **Note that**

all medications have potential side-effects and need to be prescribed and titrated very carefully.

Broad-action medications are generally the most effective to combat melancholic depression—but the risk of side-effects is highest. For this reason, if someone with melancholic depression has never taken an antidepressant before, we recommend starting with a narrow-action antidepressant and then, if there is no benefit over a couple of weeks, moving to a broader-action antidepressant or adding an augmenting medication to the antidepressant. Teenagers have an advantage in that they are more likely than adults (especially older adults with severe psychomotor disturbance) to respond to the narrower-action antidepressants.

The use of antidepressants for adolescents has evoked much controversy over the last decade. Almost certainly, most of the findings challenging their efficacy reflect their inappropriate use (especially in adolescents who do not have a melancholic depression). While melancholia is rare before mid-adolescence, we believe that antidepressant medication (and sometimes the addition of other psychotropic medication) is a key component for its treatment. The use of antidepressant medication for adolescents is overviewed in Appendix I.

Other support

Although medication is the main treatment priority for melancholic depression, it does not mean that other support isn't needed. If an adolescent has a melancholic depression, they risk consequences such as falling behind at school, and compromising friendships. It's important to address these problems with the most appropriate strategies too—via counselling, psychotherapy, or other supports.

Psychotic depression

At one level, psychotic depression is a more severe expression of melancholic depression, but with the individual also psychotic—out of touch with reality—during the worst of the episode, and experiencing delusions or hallucinations, or both.

Psychotic depression is very rare in adolescence, but clearly most important to detect. Successful management usually involves antidepressant and other medications. In adult studies of those with this condition, antidepressant medications on their own assist about 25 per cent of patients; antipsychotic medications on their own help some 33 per cent; while the combination of both medications assists about 80 per cent to achieve remission. Following remission, the antipsychotic medications can often be tapered off and ceased.

Non-melancholic depression

As noted earlier, the non-melancholic depressions reflect the interaction of stressors and/or personality styles more than a primary underlying biological problem. There are three main patterns, outlined below.

- An **acute stress-induced non-melancholic depression** is likely to occur purely as a consequence of a stressful event—like being rejected in a new relationship, or being severely bullied at school for the first time. In such instances, the adolescent feels rather like a tree that's been battered by a cyclone: they're psychologically 'flattened'. Recovery may come as a consequence of the stress (the trigger) being removed or ceasing, by the adolescent adapting, or by the adolescent processing it differently. In each of these scenarios, the stressor has thus been neutralised or negated. Many adolescents recover in this way without the need for assistance. Some, however, benefit from counselling or by learning problem-solving strategies. Antidepressant medication is rarely necessary.

- **Chronic stress-induced non-melancholic depression** is usually the result of an ongoing external stressor—one from which there is no psychological escape. For example, such depression may result from the adolescent living in a situation where he or she is constantly belittled, or continually humiliated, criticised and isolated, or bullied, or sexually abused. Here, rather like a plant that's too close to a path, the adolescent's self-esteem is exposed to constant trampling— and, over time, their capacity to spring back is diminished.

  In this case, a gardener's solution might be to move the young plant or protect it against trampling. Likewise, management of a chronic stress-induced non-melancholic depression mainly involves encouraging or contriving changes to the adolescent's social and school life, and providing support through the difficult period. Even though the cause of such depression is social, the selective serotonin reuptake inhibitor (SSRI) class of antidepressant medication can provide some relief for certain older adolescents, as they reduce the constant worrying many experience as a consequence of these stressful situations.

- The third pattern of non-melancholic depression reflects the **influence of personality on the predisposition to and the precipitation and perpetuation of a mood disorder**. An adolescent's personality can render them more vulnerable or predisposed, and make the individual more susceptible to the impact of certain stressors.

THE INFLUENCE OF PERSONALITY STYLE

Our clinical observation and research has identified **eight different personality styles** that are relevant to either predisposing, precipitating and/or perpetuating a depressive episode. These are outlined below.

- **Anxious worrying**—the teenager with such an internalising style tends to be highly strung, tense, nervy and prone to stewing over things.
- **Irritability**—a teenager with this style also tends to have high levels of trait anxiety, but they externalise their anxiety by being irritable, crabby, and easily rattled under stress.
- **Self-criticism**—a teenager with a 'self-critical' personality style tends to have low self-esteem, often reflecting a lack of parental care or even abuse in childhood, or other deprivational experiences in their early years.
- **Sensitivity to rejection**—a teenager with this personality style tends to be hypersensitive to the nuances in interpersonal relationships, and is inclined to magnify minor criticism or misinterpret others as being critical, and thus readily feels rejected and abandoned.
- **Self-focused**—the teenager with a self-focused personality style tends to lack consideration and empathy for others, is often hostile and volatile in interacting with other people, and has a low threshold for frustration.
- **Perfectionism**—a teenager with a 'perfectionistic' personality style will tend to externalise their self-image, judging their success from meeting very high standards, and if they think that they've failed to meet such high standards, or if somebody criticises their performance, they feel demeaned and crushed.
- **Socially avoidant**—a teenager with this style tends to be shy and will avoid social situations for fear of their imagined limitations being exposed, like saying something stupid, or blushing, and thereby risking ridicule.

- **Personal reserve**—a teenager with this personality style tends to be wary of others getting too close, and feels vulnerable and depressed when their inner world is exposed to others.

These personality styles are not pure types; most people who develop a personality-driven non-melancholic depression will have some combination of such styles.

The Black Dog Institute website (www.blackdoginstitute. org.au) has a Temperament and Personality Questionnaire that can be completed anonymously and provides an individual with scores on each of those personality dimensions.

The impact of personality style on mood

Let's, as an example, consider the effect of one personality style in greater detail.

Perfectionism

Adolescents with a perfectionistic personality style tend to work hard, pushing themselves to be the best. They commit themselves fully to the things they undertake. They often externalise their sense of self-worth, judging themselves by their work rather than by who they are as a person. Their perfectionism leads them to adopt very rigid and controlling behaviours. They need to be in control, and they lack the flexibility of being able to 'go with the flow'.

Perfectionistic adolescents have difficulty in trusting others—which makes it hard for them to seek help, and if they get to help, in trusting the therapist. When faced with a problem, they may judge that there are only two options at best, and often waver between the two—in a 'stable/unstable' situation—finding it impossible to consider wider options. For instance, if they are thwarted in reaching a goal, they find it difficult to either walk away from the situation or adjust to it—instead, they keep wanting to achieve their original target. Many are unable to go forward, and procrastinate to extremes. Others pour themselves into work, seeking distraction.

As perfectionistic teenagers are prone to self-criticism—but even more vulnerable to criticism from others—any criticism of their work or of other areas where they have invested their sense of self-worth risks a destructive downward spiral of depression, and obsessive, paralysing rumination about past behaviours and future decision-making.

For perfectionistic people who develop a non-melancholic depression, antidepressant medication (or any other type of medication) is rarely of any benefit. Strategies that focus on problem-solving and goal-setting can be helpful in the short term, while any long-term therapy should seek to modify their externalised self-esteem investments and aim to build up an inner identity and sense of self-worth.

Not uncommonly, perfectionistic adolescents may develop eating disorders in an attempt to control their world by controlling themselves, with the eating and depressive disorders making management difficult. This next account takes us into the world of perfectionism. It's called 'Talking About Feeling Bad'.

> I was fourteen when I began to seek isolation. I sought out silence and solitude, wandering in the early morning light with my single-lens reflex camera, studying alone in a small room, climbing trees to sit perched at the apex watching storms thunder their way across the darkened evening sky. I retreated inwards to the privacy of my own self-torment, because to share it would have meant to expose something excruciatingly tender, oddly unique.

For as long as I remember I have struggled with depression and mental illness. As a child I was kept back from school for illnesses that went undiagnosed. My lethargy led our doctor to test for Ross River fever, glandular fever, chronic fatigue syndrome; no descriptions to fit what I was feeling inside. When I was twelve, my parents separated, then divorced, leaving me a black hole to fill with tears and solitary wanderings along a mostly deserted beach. The friends I had seemed to drift away as endless moves left me feeling more and more emotionally stranded. At fourteen, my father granted me the blessing of release from the painful protocol of school. I moved with him interstate, took up studying by correspondence, and in this absence of motherly protection, schoolground persecution, and peer interaction, I let my own devils loose on myself. My bouts of mild depression turned into something much more serious.

A creative person, I began to make monsters. I drew the world as a thin crusted ball, inside of which an angel wrestled a demon. I drew little gargoyles with large claws and solemn, sad eyes. I drew loneliness sitting in a door frame, and a repentant sinner carrying a heavy sack that made him bend and stumble under the load. In my drawings I exposed anger and pain that I otherwise kept hidden. I created a dichotomous world in which good and bad existed as entirely separate and distinct realities. A world in which to triumph, one had to be completely without fault.

In an atmosphere of inner despair I had simplified my world by creating a dichotomy. I was not brave, nor wise enough to acknowledge the intricacies of human behaviour, to fathom the anomaly of emotions like love, anger, indignation, shame, fear and regret. Without a confiding ear with which to share my confusion I turned it inwards, dividing up my insides between good and bad, raging against the fear, anger and pain inside me, and attempting to eradicate all that was imperfect in my character and behaviours.

I sought out my own company because the company of others only reminded me of how bitter and bleak my world was, of how unendingly weary I was and of how sickening it was to be healthy, happy and nice.

I was literally wasted by the time I realised that I needed help. My bones stuck out from the joints at my elbows, knees and shoulders. My cheeks were hollow, my collarbone and jaw bones jutted uncannily out of my sunken face and thin chest. My thought patterns were highly destructive and I had developed a shockingly unhealthy view of myself and others. I had reached the deepest, blackest place I was ever likely to arrive at and I stood there alone, except for the agonising grasp of my favourite friend and worst enemy—the thing that sought to destroy me, the gargoyle with the sunken, solemn eyes. It gripped my body like it would never let go, invaded my mind with thoughts only of how terrible I looked, of how much of a burden I was to others and of how much easier it would be to just slip away.

But slipping away was not an option. Nor was coping in that self-inflicted hell. I knew I had to find a way out. Instinct told me to return to formal schooling, so I enrolled myself in Year 12 at a high school in another state. My father and brothers moved with me, and for the first time in five years I was faced with having to build relationships with my peers. I found myself yearning to be treated as one of them and to be accepted by them, regardless of my inward awkwardness.

The year was 1999 and I remember it as the year of my parents' anger and tears. I sought medical assistance at an adolescent service, seeing a doctor who attempted to counsel me as well as to prescribe antidepressants which I would not take. I attended regular meetings of a group of young people suffering a range of disorders and sat silently mulling, afraid to speak lest I say something stupid or get caught in the tangle of my inner emotions. I tried to be discreet at school and spent most of my time alone, but someone in my literature class sought me out in the playground and made herself my friend. I continued to feel despondent, hopeless and full of self-loathing at home, and despite all my attempts at becoming healthy, I lost even more weight.

Years passed in constant struggle with myself, my thoughts and my emotions. Feelings kept surfacing that I did not understand and had no control over. I cried for hours over emotions that I did not know I had—feelings of abandonment, grief at my inability to feel love for myself or from others, abysmal loneliness and the grief of not having a solid family unit to turn to for help. I would walk the streets restless and inconsolable over a small argument with housemates about cleanliness. I refused to see people in my life who had made me feel bad, or any worse than I already did.

I was riding a rollercoaster on which the power kept coming on and off so that I would be left for long periods dangling dangerously over an edge, or slide back into a dipper after climbing halfway up. I saw a psychotherapist, two psychologists, a naturopath, and a doctor turned counsellor by turn. The only one with any decent advice was the doctor, who suggested I do three things—fail a subject, start dating, and try everything that wasn't dangerous or illegal. The most difficult thing was reaching out to someone who could help when I most needed it.

After years of feeling unconfident and putting myself down, I decided to take possession. I forced myself to join university clubs, lead orientation two years in a row, became involved in a local church, took a drawing class on Monday nights and started to study a language. After a year of learning Hebrew, I decided to take a trip to the Middle East and bought myself a return ticket to Istanbul. There I started to suffer panic attacks before language class in the mornings and, after some reflection, discovered that my expectations of myself were far too high. I began to learn the lessons that my doctor had taught: not to fear failure and not to remain aloof, striving for that unreachable aim of having a flawless character.

At some stage I started to make concrete decisions about how I wanted to be—as a friend, partner, daughter, niece, granddaughter, sister, aunt, student, employee. My family, I realised, meant the world to me and my friends were like life-lines that I reached out to continually. I began to feel things again which I hadn't allowed myself to feel for a long time: indignation, anger, shame, love, sympathy, regret and fear. At first these emotions were difficult to deal with, but it became easier with time, and as I released emotions that I had stored for years, I became happier and healthier.

My experience of depression has been dominated by a more powerful disorder known as anorexia nervosa. It is a disorder driven by depression—an isolating, debilitating, selfish and life-threatening illness. In overcoming this illness, and tackling the accompanying depression, my task was to create a healthy self-esteem. That is, an ability to judge my capacities in an honest manner, so that when I saw myself in my mind's eye, I was not a reflection of someone else, nor an incarnation of all that I hated or loathed.

I had to learn to treat myself with kindness, to learn to experience and express emotion, to be independent and yet dependent and able to stand alone as well as to share in the joys and struggles of humanity. When I see myself or spend time with myself alone now, I am no longer engulfed by a tide of animosity or a barrage of self-berating thoughts. I am able to feel love towards myself and others. **Rosa**

Here is another story, perhaps illustrating the interaction between personality style (shyness and personal reserve) and stressful events. Shy adolescents tend to be unassertive and are often bullied or have their needs ignored. Here the shyness is apparent, as are a series of stressful events resulting from this girl's treatment by others (father, best friend, teacher), who are variously demeaning, rejecting, bullying and dismissive of her.

This extract, and the one following, illustrate aspects of a **reactive** depression—where the stress of circumstances further exacerbates each teenager's depression.

This is Girl's story. It could be any Girl. Anywhere. Your friend. Your child. You.

As the second-youngest of six children, Girl found it easy to feel lost amongst the commotion of family life. Girl started to experience 'dark moods' as the constant referral to her as 'the quiet, shy sister of ...' took its toll. Once Girl hit her teen years, it became harder and harder for her to contain her ever-changing emotions. Huge fights would erupt between Girl and her father, the commotion finally coming to an end with Girl screaming alone in her bedroom, trying desperately to rid herself of her dark rage.

Used to being called 'quiet and reserved' by teachers and strangers, Girl knew she could rely on her friends to see the 'real' her: funny, witty, smart and someone who would never tell a secret. They were her safety net—the thread holding her together. This thin thread snapped in early Year 12. Girl overheard her best friend describing her as 'the girl who's always in the corner'. That was all that was needed for Girl's fragile safety net to fail her and she felt herself plummeting, fast. She was seventeen.

Girl never recovered from that fall. She severed all ties from her friends as her days grew darker and darker. Her sleeping patterns became increasingly erratic, switching from being unable to sleep at night and wanting to sleep all day, to falling asleep as soon as she returned home from school, utterly exhausted. Nothing interested her anymore and she was constantly crying. Consumed by her inner battle, Girl didn't recognise that those around her had noticed the change in her too. Girl's mother had noticed a steady decline in her self-esteem and a withdrawal from her usual activities.

It was also during this time that Girl fell in love with and started a relationship with a fellow student. Another girl. Due to attending a Catholic senior high school, problems initially started when the other students found out. This continued with the teachers discovering Girl's 'secret'. Girl felt no support or care from those she was told she could count on. She experienced name-calling while in public places, rumours, having rotten fruit thrown at her and being spat on.

Girl stewed over it for a long time before finally gathering up the courage to confide in a teacher she felt she could trust to give her advice and somewhere to turn. At that time, Girl felt she had no options and was completely alone. Girl was filled with hope when this teacher seemed to react positively to her plight. She said she would soon get back to her with some helpful information and left Girl feeling somewhat hopeful.

Not only did this teacher never get back to Girl with any information, she avoided her for the rest of the year. Girl retreated further and further into her own little world—fearful to let anyone too close for fear of further hurt and humiliation. **Genevieve**

This next extract provides another example of a reactive depression—a depressive episode that can be largely explained as a consequence of living with major stressors.

A tumultuous childhood of divorced parents, blended with my sensitive, pensive and analytical personality, mixed with a highly delicate biochemistry, and a pinch of destiny to taste, left a young woman like myself susceptible to an emotional and mental breakdown. However, in hindsight and with the knowledge of what can be gained by experiencing such hardships, I would call these times a breakthrough. **Jasmine**

What follows next is the story of a young boy living with the anguish of an undiagnosed depression, the depression itself being probably secondary to the anxiety disorder sub-type of obsessive compulsive disorder (OCD).

When I was about ten years old I began my 'worrying'. It included various things at different times—checking clothing inside and out for spiders, regular and obsessive handwashing, assigning relevance to particular numbers and repeating actions a number of times to multiples of those numbers until it 'felt right'. This went on for a few years. As I became more frustrated I began to hit myself in the forehead with the base of my palm whenever I got too caught up in my obsessive compulsions. Well aware, though, of how my physically obvious obsessions might look, I eventually learnt to deal with many of them and not be seen to be acting weirdly.

I was lucky enough to maintain a natural stubbornness to never let this 'worrying' get in the way of important things in my life. And throughout my adolescence my friends became the most important thing for me, and provided the moments when I felt most at ease and anxiety-free. At high school I was able to hide my anxiety and obsessiveness pretty well. Though incredibly shy and lacking in self-confidence for a long time, I appeared like any other kid to teachers, the other kids, family and friends.

In a way I'd liberated myself to live a normal teenage life by being able to fit in somewhat, but I hadn't dealt with the cause of my problems and my anxiety disorder continued. The obsession with particular numbers was subtle enough to continue, as did other obsessive thoughts, relating largely to religious and superstitious fears. The exact worries and irrational thoughts I had were varied and ever-changing, but were largely irrelevant to discussion of the essential problem. I had times of crippling fear and anxiety, and the more I continued to give in to it, through obsessive thoughts and rituals, the worse it got.

That I made it through school was an achievement in itself. That I was able to achieve the marks to get into university was purely down to the fact I just figured some things had to be done, and I am extremely grateful now that I was able to. I don't know how I managed to focus like that when I absolutely needed to, but I was extremely lucky. **Harrison**

In summary, it is very relevant for a therapist to consider personality style and its contribution when assessing a mood disorder. The interaction of temperament and environment (which results in 'personality') colours and shapes the mood disorder, and the effectiveness of any intervention, and longer-term management plans, might depend on framing therapy to fit with the individual's personality-based views and ways of interacting with the world.

BIPOLAR DISORDER

In addition to the three broad expressions of depression covered earlier, a significant percentage of teenagers develop a **bipolar disorder** (Type I or II, as described before), with onset common in high school.

The depressive episodes that are the downswings of bipolar disorder tend to be psychotic (rarely) or melancholic (mainly), although several of the classic melancholic symptoms experienced by adults are either not evident or manifest quite differently in adolescence. While adults tend to experience early morning wakening, and appetite and weight loss, teenagers with melancholia (and especially those with a bipolar condition) are more likely to develop atypical symptoms of hypersomnia (sleeping excessively) and hyperphagia (eating excessively).

Such symptoms are not specific to bipolar disorder—also being common in many young people under stress, and especially those with a personality style of sensitivity to rejection—and may reflect compensatory homeostatic (self-righting) mechanisms in the stressed or non-melancholically depressed teenager.

Management of bipolar disorder

We suggest that management of bipolar disorder involves four key features:

- medication
- education
- counselling
- the development of a wellbeing plan.

Medication options are not detailed here but may involve the use of antidepressant medication, mood stabilisers and even antipsychotic medications at times—especially for individuals with Bipolar I.

Education helps to promote the individual's sense of control over the condition—to move from feeling *controlled by* the condition to having *control over* it and thus not being defined by the condition. There are many books about bipolar disorder and many excellent and informative websites. However, most educational material is in relation to Bipolar I, and there is little in relation to the more commonly occurring Bipolar II. The Black Dog Institute has therefore developed an internet-delivered 'Bipolar Disorder Education Program', and produced a book for clinicians and researchers about Bipolar II.[3]

Counselling further assists the teenager to come to terms with a bipolar illness and learn how to manage it successfully. A diagnosis of bipolar disorder is almost invariably a shock to a teenager's sense of identity, and they may fear the impact that it could have on their life. Mental illness poses a threat to study plans, career and finding a life partner, and counselling can help the young person work through such issues.

Good supportive counselling for bipolar disorder should explore how the teenager feels about the diagnosis and provide information about resources. It should help the teenager work through any losses the illness has entailed, help them rebuild their sense of self, and assist them to maintain supportive close relationships.

While our plan for managing bipolar disorder involves many different avenues of support (medication, education and counselling), we would emphasise that young people with any type of mood disorder usually benefit from a multi-faceted approach, rather than being offered medication only. We will look at how to develop a wellbeing plan in greater detail in Chapter 8.

The following story is from Amy, who developed a bipolar disorder in early adolescence, and who then progressively mastered the condition by learning to 'control it' and by effectively developing her own wellbeing plan. While individual strategies will have differing results for differing individuals, there is a common message for those teenagers who have to deal—and do in fact learn to deal—with a chronic or intermittent mood disorder. Amy titles her story 'The Devil and Me'.

This story is for everybody out there suffering. For anybody who has ever looked around and thought, 'What a crazy bizarre world. *Am I missing something here?*' For people who think they may be crazy. For those who struggle in the dungeons of their own mind. For those who have trouble coping with life and just don't know why …

For as long as I can remember, I have had a niggling feeling that something was 'wrong', something was different about me. I remember it clearly in childhood, and this intensified considerably throughout my adolescence and my early youth. When I look back on my adolescence, my memories are surrounded by a grey fog, and tinged with sadness. Many times I convinced myself that I just wanted to be 'different', that there was nothing at all wrong with me. It's like listening to a symphony of beautiful music with just a few notes off—it's hard to put your finger on it, but you know that something is wrong.

On countless occasions I struggled with daily life—it's as if someone had tied a brick around my heart and was daring me to swim. The slow suffocation and strangulation of despair would descend upon me, like a parachute gracefully landing. I could often see it coming, and try to brace myself. Other times, it fell upon me quicker than a swift kick in the guts. It is not enough to just say 'snap out of it'. I would want to, and try my damn hardest to—but it was me against the Devil. And the Devil often won. He would take me to highs and lows like never before. Sometimes I felt privileged—no-one else had seen the wonders from the heights I had climbed. The Devil was my best friend, the only constant friend I'd known. I didn't know any better.

But for every time I soared upon the wind, there was an immediate plummet into the prison that was my own dark mind. And you never knew just how long or severe my sentence was. I once heard that the Devil's most sinister trick was to trick people into not believing him. In floods of endless tears, and bloodied self-mutilation on my arms, I would often ask: 'Is this all there is?' And more often than not, I was convinced that yes, this was life, just the best it could get. To ask for more would be ungrateful.

My demon had convinced me he did not even exist.

The constant guilt that I felt from being depressed, sometimes about nothing, would hang off my shoulders. In these times, the Devil would be a harsh and pervasive voice, preaching to me the *shoulds* and *should nots* of how I should be feeling. When you add a serving of guilt and self-doubt to the already utter despair of depression, it is a recipe for suicide.

For many lucky people, 'depression' and 'bipolar' are but vague words. It is almost impossible to understand what it truly feels like unless you have struggled on that dark road yourself. I remember waking up in the mornings, and feeling like someone heavy was sitting on my chest. At other times, I could not shut down my mind, no matter how hard I tried. The adrenaline would cause me to get overexcited and do the sorts of things people would do when they were drunk.

Most of all, there was the daily struggle between the mood disorder Devil and myself. We were in a toxic, unhealthy relationship. The arguments were constant, with no relief in my mind. They would often last long into the night. I could not 'shut down', and sleep was a luxury. I would often stare out of my virtual cage with longing and envy at all the lucky, normal people, who just 'got it', in life.

These days that intense depression feels like another world, a twilight zone … Hell, sometimes I can hardly even remember what it feels like, until, on occasion, the Devil makes an unexpected and uninvited house call. He tries to convince me of the euphoric times we had together. But now I know better. Those moments dissolve as quickly as sugar in boiling hot tea.

And they leave burn marks. Forever.

So, how did I learn to finally break it off with the Devil, and bask in the warm sunshine of life? It all happened one very ordinary day. For years I'd had suspicions that my depression and extreme moods were a problem 'outside' of myself. Kind of like being born blind, or without a leg. No-one can really help this. Years of reading, counselling, meditation, church and much more pointed out that I had tried my best—and that this was not enough. This illness *is not my fault.* I am not to blame. Those hours spent researching in the high school library finally came to fruition. The acceptance of bipolar disorder with its downs and ups as a proper, classifiable illness has been for me the INSTRUMENTAL first step in getting me back on the path I was always meant to be on.

By finally accepting bipolar disorder as an *outside* defect, it opened the doors to the mysterious world of healing. Medication made an entry into my life, and has been MONUMENTAL in balancing my struggle with the Devil. If I were born with one leg, medication has given me the other leg, so that I can simply compete equally in the game of life. I am no longer disabled. And this is all I ask for. My fear of medication turning me into a 'fake and boring' person has melted away. I have become *more* of myself, and not less.

And I still have my edge.

The journey to healing and recovery is definitely a marathon event. It will never be the 100-metre sprint. Alongside my marathon, I have discovered the GROW program to support my mental health. This idea was a visitor in my mind that I constantly ignored. And then one day I opened the door. Now that door is always open. The first few visits were hard. I wanted to bolt my door shut and pretend I was permanently out. But the GROW program, and its members, have cleaned out my mind, heart and soul, and given me a shiny new perspective. It has also given me the opportunity to support others who are in similar boats on the same ocean. In this support group, I can truly B R E A T H E !

I once heard an insightful quote: 'You alone can do it, but you cannot do it alone.' I'll never in my life forget the night that my own family members FINALLY took me seriously about my illness. They had never really understood it, and were not necessarily willing to. It took hours of soul-baring and conversations deep into the night. But finally, here was my mother, after all these years, loving me and accepting me with watery eyes. She was actually proud of me, and what I had been through. My mum and sisters opened their eyes and saw all my different sides and angles, under the harsh light of the truth. And I was a sparkling diamond.

What then naturally flowed into my life was the ability to see myself as a fragile piece of glass, and take care of myself delicately. I become drained very easily, and my energy is very sensitive. You could say that I am like a mobile phone that constantly needs to be charged, otherwise it will run out of battery very quickly! What recharges me is regular, sweaty exercise. Good food. Lots of time alone. Regular naps. Time with nature. Getting rid of outside 'noise'. The noise of the world.

I imagine my mind as a large dark cave, with a 24/7 guard standing out the front. His job is to fight away negative thoughts, unproductive feelings, and any other dangerous stimuli. There are times when my guard has fallen asleep on the job, and occasionally, he has gone on holidays without any notice! But I am getting there. He is getting better and better at from afar spotting the return of the Devil.

I see myself as a very expensive car that needs to run on premium petrol in order to function optimally. I am very careful with myself. For example, too much time alone can be isolating. And for someone with a mood disorder, isolation is as easy and comfortable to slip into as a warm coat on a chilly winter's night.

I'm a high-maintenance girl—but I'm worth it.

There are no more struggles between the Devil and me. I have seen beauty that no-one else can see.

Instead of black, grey and white, my world is now in full, splendid technicolour. **Amy**

This next extract is the 'happy ending' of Cam's story, a world away from its sombre beginnings in Chapter 1 of this book. Cam and his parents effectively accessed help and their shift in attitude—from initially dreading mental health intervention to their very effective use of it—is inspiring. The rest of Shelley and Cam's story illustrates the support they received from so many different sources: their extended family; the doctor who had known Cam since childhood (and we see evidence here of some earlier difficulties that Cam had overcome); the effective and immediate referral to an appropriate health care professional; the initial usefulness of medication to help Cam out of the trough; and sensitive assistance from the school. Together with the ever-present optimism and support of his parents, this network of care has restored Cam nearly back to his old self.

Cam's parents were also aware of the impact of his mood disorder on the rest of their children, and by being available and open to them, helped to alleviate the starvation that can result when one family member in acute need is consuming all the available emotional food.

And so we now continue with Shelley's story, 'A Child Dissolves'.

> ... There were many phone calls to my mother and sister who were very supportive and understanding, but at this stage I was so upset on a daily basis that I could hardly complete a conversation without crying. We were desperate, alone and struggling to connect with our once happy, loving child who was now an empty shell walking around with this black cloud hovering over him and walls so thick surrounding him no-one could get in. We were all breaking under the pressure.

Cam had been under the care of a wonderful paediatrician since he was about five years old (due to some learning and social difficulties), and we decided that a visit was well overdue. We had our consultation with the doctor, and after about ten minutes of speaking one-on-one to Cam, he asked him to wait outside in the waiting room, so he was able to speak with me alone. The minute the door closed, the doctor turned to me and said, 'Shelley, that must be breaking your heart!' I dissolved into tears (which was just about a daily occurrence now and they were just below the surface, always) and started to tell him the complete story. He understood, agreed with me, and we began to get some concrete things in place. He stated that it would be a long road back. I replied, 'Whatever it takes' and truly meant it. I would have given anything and everything to get him back. I did not know it would be possible then. He suggested immediate intervention to our local hospital, to a specialist psychologist who deals with teenage clinical depression. He was so concerned at the state our son was in, he wrote the referral, and rang the doctor then and there; we went straight to our local hospital that day.

Cam, his dad and I attended our first consultation, where he was officially diagnosed with clinical depression. This came as more of a confirmation than a shock for us. But now, what to do? The doctor recommended medication, along with eight sessions of therapy. We took both.

At first the change was subtle—things like our son coming out at 6 p.m. and sitting with us to eat, not saying much, but just being there. We were all shell-shocked, we trod on eggshells and talked about everything else but what was happening.

My husband found it very difficult to speak with Cam on the same level as I did: I was the one who would sit in his room and have long conversations with him, bring him late night 'cuppas' and sit and chat, trying to tactfully explain why the way he acted was not right, or why what he said could be hurtful. Offering support on a daily basis so he could keep up with schoolwork. Helping with practical stuff, like organising his room and clothes. Explaining it from another's point of view, because he just couldn't see how his actions could be hurtful. Pleading with him to talk to us. Constantly plugging in to his life, forcing him to communicate. That's what it means to be a mother ... you just don't/can't give up.

My husband started spending time with him, just doing what he (Cam) wanted to do. Most evenings they would stay up late using the Playstation, or listening to comedy CDs, whatever, it didn't matter, they were connecting anyway. They interacted through the characters in the games, connected through the jokes on the CDs and became close again—all the while never speaking about depression or the issues at hand. It was his 'role' to be a father/friend. The interactions and time spent was one of fun and relaxation, no pressure, it evolved into a wonderful, close father/son bond once again. They just did it in a different fashion than I would have. Men and boys, I have learnt, don't talk about 'issues', they talk about 'stuff'. It's almost like it's in the too-hard basket for men to broach, so they just don't. But by using the 'around the hedge' approach they still get the job done. It's just more subtle.

I cut back on work, and took Cam to weekly sessions at our local hospital for therapy. We continued medication and very slowly we started to see small changes grow into medium changes. We were apprehensive of course, but what was the alternative? You just can't sit back and watch your child disappear.

I wrote to the school counsellor to ask for additional support from the school. This was perhaps the hardest thing to do, because I wrote one of those four-page letters straight from the heart, explaining what Cam had been through this year, and that we as his family were at a crisis point; not knowing at the time whether it would fall on deaf ears or not. Luckily for us, our local school was very supportive and offered additional help with tuition support at school, and also looked to rework his timetable to alleviate the stress with keeping up with certain subjects that were simply beyond him at this stage.

Our salvation finally came in the form of Donna, the Special Ed Support Unit Teacher newly employed by the school to help 'integrate and support' those students with extra needs. The school counsellor asked my permission to allow Donna to read my letter, because she felt it would bring Donna up to speed in a way she could not. I allowed it, but asked for confidentiality as Cam's feelings and wellbeing was our number one concern.

We met with Donna, and things turned around for our son from that day onwards. She helped educate teachers to find a better way to deal with students that were 'a square peg in a round hole'. She helped alleviate some of the stress, with timetabling and deadlines—she set up a system where Cam goes to her three times each week for tutorial lessons, where she offers study support, organisation support, computer access. In short, she is his 'safe haven' at school.

This didn't happen overnight. Initially Cam was resentful at being seen as 'different' and didn't accept any help or support, but after those few months he is now comfortable to accept help and is a happy, upbeat, productive student once again. All of a sudden, top marks take a back seat in our house—we just want him to get through the day, and do his best, whatever that is.

Depression was never something I thought I would have to deal with from this angle, and having a child so seriously affected is truly confronting. The guilt is overwhelming: you blame yourself, thinking there must have been something you had or hadn't done, or not noticed, but I now know that sometimes it just happens—no matter how much you love your child, no matter how close you are.

I believe it was a culmination of a number of things for Cam: not fitting in at school, struggling with maintaining good grades, the pressure of assignments and schoolwork (with a learning disability), self-esteem issues.

What I would say to parents is, never give up, simply never. No matter how many fights, screaming matches, bad grades, phone calls from school. Your child is still in there and you can find them again. I am thankful every day for the health care professionals who listened and took us seriously. I'm thankful for the medication that makes a difference. I'm thankful for good teachers (and yes, there were some that were not helpful at all), but for those few who really do make a difference, you are worth your weight in gold, and are important to those kids that struggle, and you are helping to make their school life bearable. But most importantly, I am thankful for family, because nothing tests you like Depression, and it is that support that will get them and us through.

We now have our fifteen-year-old back from a very dark place; he attends school (happily), has a small social group, and goes out on weekends, keeps up with most of his schoolwork, does odd jobs around the house for pocket money.

Really ... what more could you want? **Shelley**

To sum up

The successful resolution of, and recovery from, a mood disorder is most likely to be achieved when the treatment is appropriately matched to the drivers and causes of the particular condition. For this reason there is a very clear need to establish the type of mood disorder and to then initiate a management plan that addresses its underlying causes, in a manner that is suited to the individual.

. . . .

A FRAMEWORK FOR ACTION

Assisting strong self-management habits plays a central role in bringing mood disorders under control.

The importance of medication compliance

If the young person has been prescribed medication, compliance is a potential concern. A lot of people—and especially adolescents—don't like taking medication, particularly prophylactic medication that's needed to prevent another episode of bipolar or depressive illness. Also be aware that the side-effects of medication can sometimes occur before its benefits. For these reasons it is not uncommon for individuals to question why they should continue to take medication that doesn't seem to do anything for them day-to-day. Regrettably, it may take repeated episodes of an illness before an individual will decide to continue with medication, even if it has been clearly shown to be beneficial.

Three golden rules
If a teenager is taking medication for a mood disorder there are three essential rules you must always remember.

- They should be regularly monitored and have ready access to their doctor. The doctor should also have in place effective support arrangements for any period that the doctor is unavailable.
- It is extremely important *not* to come off medication until the psychiatrist or GP advises that stopping it is okay.
- Most antidepressant medications *should not be ceased abruptly* as withdrawal effects can be very severe.

A teenager who has been prescribed antidepressant medication should tell their parents and their doctor if they notice any bad side-effects (such as severe agitation, palpitations, insomnia).

Decide who's responsible for what

It's important to agree about who takes responsibility for each management step. For example, the teenager in your care agrees that you can contact the medical facility or the doctor if you judge that they are unwell. These agreements are best made ahead of time, when the young person is well and potential levels of conflict are low.

Identify periods of high vulnerability

Some teenagers with bipolar disorder—and those with melancholic depression—may find that their **mood becomes unstable seasonally, especially in spring**.

Early warning signs should be identified, as there are often similar 'signatures' across episodes. **Disrupted sleep is a common marker of the beginning of an episode.** These early warning signs can be communicated to trusted others, so that the teen has an extra level of cushioning. This has been called 'outside insight'—an objective view that is especially valuable in the case of any loss of insight by the young person.

Consider the timing of interventions

Individuals with bipolar disorder commonly avoid or resist help because they enjoy the highs. They are more motivated to seek help during the depressed phase of their illness, but most likely to agree on an action plan in between episodes.

The answer is information, and yet more information

It's really important to access as much information as possible so that you can read about research-based management strategies and what resources are available for helping a teenager to live with a mood disorder. Keep up with the latest findings. The internet is a very rich resource (provided the information comes from a reliable website), and it is accessible on your local library computer if technology is not your forte or discretion is needed.

Supporting the young person

Teenagers (and anyone) are likely to feel invaded when you talk with them about their mental health. Be sensitive. Pick your time. There are subtle ways to make information available for their further education. Maybe you can leave information sheets or sympathetic easy-to-read books about the subject in an accessible place. This information could include a list of reputable websites that the young person is able to access themselves.

Other things you can do for them

- Instead of talking, just listen, without leaping in with advice.
- Go with them to their appointments if possible; maybe make time for a coffee afterwards.
- Try to make things a little easier for them: offer them a lift to the library if they're studying, support them with some resources, help with photocopying, internet searches etc.

- Discuss strategies for time management; try to spot and relieve other stressors.
- Encourage them to exercise—make time for it.
- Do something together that might be a shared interest: start a photo album, encourage them to keep a box of their special things (awards, cards from friends, mementos and such).
- Help them to recognise the triggers and early warning signs of a mood swing—then agree on a course of action; don't ignore the signs.
- Encourage them, and continue searching with them, to find the right professional support.

Matthew and Ainsley Johnstone—to whom we're indebted for the above suggestions—in their very helpful book *Living with a Black Dog*[4] advise taking a united front and getting M.A.D. 'M' is for management, 'A' is for acceptance and 'D' is for discipline.

Constantly review the management plan

A management plan will include several strategies. For depression, it may be to help the adolescent change their negative thinking patterns or problem behaviours, or to address stresses in relationships that may be contributing to their mood swings. A health care professional can also help the adolescent and his or her parents and caregivers recognise early warning signs of depression and/or a bipolar high, and teach strategies to prevent or control further episodes.

When the management plan fails

What to do when things go wrong and self-management habits go belly up? Or, despite the best efforts of all, another depressive or bipolar episode occurs?

The important thing is to try not to point the finger and say, 'Well, you should have done this', or 'The doctor should have done that'. It's much more important to think about what contributed to the slip, and then to re-establish management and containment plans.

It is also essential that these plans are adapted to suit the young person, and are not just left as vague ideals: together, look at their lifestyle and habits and negotiate what is necessary around their routines and interests. Update and adapt; drop activities or commitments that simply aren't working.

. . . .

8. Maintaining good mental health

Tips from teens and their supporters

Slowly, piece by piece, I cobbled together my own
headspace: chance encounters with peers who were
doing their best, like me, to keep their struggles hidden;
words like balm from a few sympathetic adults and
allies: 'I'm on your side,' 'I like the way you think,'
'Trust …' Help also came via the school library.
In time I was able to uncurl and notice things in the
world outside. Once, lining up at the chemist, I was
surprised and reassured to see a boy with the same
medication as me. It was a revelation that he looked
no different to any other boy. In a moment of solidarity,
some of the fear and shame dissipated. **Mitchell**

My secret—recognise that you're not a social misfit and that
great people also have been bullied and ridiculed as kids.
Great people all too often did not come from the expected
'stable' family environment—great people are often born
from the ashes of adversity! **Sean**

While recovery from a mood disorder may be 'like a
cha-cha—one step forward, two steps back',[1] early intervention

brings rewards. Teenagers have resilience and flexibility and generally more fluid options open to them than those who are older. Many teenagers emerge from the throes of a mood disorder wiser than their age and with a maturity and a level of compassion and empathy that is not always the hallmark of adolescence. This grace is also reflected in their willingness to accept support from others, as seen in the story below.

On Tuesday he goes to see Andrew. He tells Andrew about how he's been feeling. He tells him about the thoughts that bubble and gurgle in his mind. He tells him all the things, good and bad, that he's been longing to say to people. He talks about love and joy. He talks about anger and frustration.

He talks.

When the 50 minutes are up, he ventures back into the world outside his head. There's a cool breeze and a radiant pink sky. These things strengthen him. He walks home and puts on some music. He sings along this time, and puts his heart into it. He doesn't worry about whether or not anyone can hear him. The words force their way out onto the air, each one carrying away a tiny crumb of pain.

He knows that sometimes people just have to get on with things. But he knows that people are sometimes so busy getting on with things they forget to take care of themselves. He knows this is what he has done. If only someone had told him he had to make himself fully functional before he could be of use to anyone else.

Later that year, he gives a speech to a big group of students. He tells them honestly about what he experienced and how he hopes none of them ever have to go through it. He tells them that if they do have to deal with pain, that it's important they don't see it as the end, but rather as a step towards being a better human. By telling his story, by sharing his pain, and seeing it for what it is—depression—he takes control. **Josh**

Our next contributor, referring to his depressive disorder as his 'black dog', shares humorous and astute tips about what he has found helpful in managing his ongoing depressive disorder. His pluralistic approach—taking what he needs from a range of options—has worked for him.

Twelve years on, there is a lot I wish I'd known at 22. Medication helps a great deal, but managing depression—in the short or the long term—is generally a more complex and individual game. At 22, my black dog was a gigantic, slobbering doberman that slept on my bed during the night and followed me everywhere I went. Now I have a scottie that mostly sleeps outside in his kennel. I still have to take him to obedience classes, but sometimes I can leave him at home.

Here's what I've learned about managing my black dog:

- Tell your close friends and family about your pet: they may notice he is getting bigger and developing bad habits before you do.
- Read your dog books about Zen, particularly the parts about acceptance. Read him Harry Potter books, particularly the funny bits.
- Find a canine-friendly GP and take your dog along for regular check-ups (particularly after an initial diagnosis, or if you've just started taking medication).
- Recognise that black dogs choose their owners, not the other way around. The black dog will pick anyone it wants to, irrespective of age, gender or intellect (and he

doesn't care whether you believe in him or not).

- Take your dog to the park: sit in a stripy deckchair in the sun.
- Never ask your black dog for his opinion: while he may seem convincing, he often makes very bad decisions.
- Get your dog a timetable: even if the only structure in your days are regular sleeping times, go out for a newspaper after lunch and a quick game of 'fetch' before dinner.
- Keep an eye out for other black dog owners: they pop up in the most unexpected places and often have good training tips.
- Take your dog to visit people you know well and places where you feel safe. Take him to play with children you like.
- Getting angry and yelling at your black dog's bad behaviour rarely helps, but if you consistently speak to him in a firm voice he will eventually learn.
- Black dogs hate water: have a bath, go swimming, sit by the river or walk along the beach without your shoes.
- If you suspect that someone you know lives with a big black dog, don't assume they know, because sometimes he hides behind the lounge.
- I've learned that what you are feeling isn't always what other people expect you to be feeling, and this is okay. Scrambled eggs is better than no dinner at all.
- Trust your instincts to help choose a psychiatrist or psychologist: they need to understand you and you need to trust them.
- Finally, understand that you will be okay one day, although that day might not be today.

I'm all right now, more or less. My scottie still lives with me but after lots of training he's generally fairly well behaved. **Mick**

The following excerpts are from people who relate their varying experiences of who and what helped them to recover and to maintain that recovery.

To me, my son David is famous. David gets out of bed every morning. He chose to live when he had so many reasons not to. But he would never have made it if he hadn't trusted those around him—teachers, headmaster, friends, family, his psychologist and especially his psychiatrist. Teenagers want to be normal. They often hide behind this mask. It is hard to help them when you can't reach their soul. David laid his soul open and grabbed many outstretched hands. His dream now is to offer his hand, especially to teenagers, those who lose their childhoods, lose their lives. In his brother's honour, he wants to help prevent other meaningless deaths. **Liza**

Since my hospital experience, I had resisted counselling but I gave this psychologist a chance. At the first session, something he said really made me feel quite happy. He said that I should see my overdose as a 'hiccup' and try to stop thinking about it. He taught me how to relax using relaxation techniques. After attending several sessions, I felt good—but not fixed. I was happy seeing him, but I looked up to him as a grandfather figure, not someone who I could tell all of my feelings to. He understood, and referred me to another psychologist who he thought was best for me.

My first session with her was good. After hearing my story, she diagnosed me with depression: I finally felt that I knew what was wrong and that I wasn't crazy. She recommended antidepressants and contacted my GP the next day. I continue seeing her regularly. I feel that I have someone who listens and won't hold anything against me. She is teaching me how to deal with arguments and bad situations and how to react to them without hurting myself.

After experiencing many unpleasant situations that resulted in 'episodes' as I now call them, I have started to understand more about my condition and to cope with thoughts of suicide when they come. I also experience thoughts about tattooing myself for an adrenaline rush. She is helping me deal with such thoughts.

The medication has also helped me. I have been on it for four months. I believe it gives me time to think before I react impulsively in bad situations. My mum was hesitant about me taking antidepressants as it is not recommended for under-18s, but she asked other doctors about it and supported my wish to give the tablets a try. I don't know how long it will take me to get off these but in the future I would like to stop relying on them. **Rowan**

It has taken time, faith and the invaluable support of my family, friends and practitioners to keep the severest of my dark moods at bay and most importantly, to keep me safe when I may be a threat to myself.

Often I have been too unwell to make my own decisions, therefore it is important to have people around you whom you trust enough to see that the treatment is in your best interest. I have also been blessed with members of my family who took it upon themselves to seek their own education about depression. I have not once felt a burden to them. They have shared the role of helping me and continuously touch base with my doctors to see how things are progressing. This interaction and continuity of care is very important and provides a sense of stability during times of uncertainty and fragility.

And the individuality of my friends shines through as their presence is often not so much focused on the depression, but upon the lighter aspects in life, making sure that socialising, sharing meals, seeing movies, writing letters and long talks late into the night continue to be part of my life, even when I have little vitality. Knowing that they know of my vulnerabilities is a comfort in itself.

This support network provides me with differing assistance, yet I know that they are all there to see that I can improve my health and learn to manage the more challenging moments. A naturopath friend may have different beliefs to my psychiatrist, and one psychologist may encourage me to use my art as a means for expression and healing, while an avid meditator suggests I simply meditate on my breath. I have chosen to embrace all these ideas and rather than force myself to stringently adopt every rule in the book, I have integrated and found within myself what works best for me. We are, as it stands, our own greatest healer.

Over the years, as I have matured and become more self-aware, I have discovered that there is no single treatment to alleviate the mental suffering I have experienced in life. Separating the mind from the body from the soul is impossible. We are multi-faceted beings and until I opened up beyond medicinal treatment and found the confidence to talk to therapists and take responsibility for my problems, to educate myself with the basic needs for my body that would maintain my health, i.e. nutrition, exercise and a drug-and-alcohol-free lifestyle, to befriend myself, to care for my soul and find what truly makes me happy, only then did I begin to believe that, despite the excruciating pain one can suffer, there are many gifts and insights waiting for us on the other side of despair.

The most salient message I wish to share with others

is to simply encourage them to make some form of communication when the mind takes over, whatever the nature of the thought—be it self-threatening, aggressive, morbid, berating, helpless or sinister. Regardless, it cannot be feared when spoken of in the company of someone who will acknowledge it.

Over time, society is becoming more aware of the prevalence of mood disorders, and just as prevalent are the people and resources willing to support the cause. Expelling what one can muster from the inside out is a liberating experience, and the first step in removing yourself from the bite of the black dog. From there on in, all wounds can be soothed and healed. **Jasmine**

Following is a brief overview of some of the psychological therapies our teens have mentioned as being of help in managing their mood disorders.

A PROFESSIONAL, SYMPATHETIC EAR

On their own, the therapies outlined below are unlikely to be of major benefit in cases of melancholic or psychotic depression, but they may assist if used in conjunction with medication.

Cognitive behaviour therapy (CBT)

Young people with depression often have an ongoing negative view of themselves (even when they are not depressed), and distort their experiences through a negative filter. Their thinking patterns may be so habitual that they don't even notice the errors in their judgment, everyday assumptions and interpretations that are caused by thinking irrationally.

In the sequence **event–thought–reaction**, most people aren't aware of the step in the middle: *thought*. These habits of mind usually aren't a problem unless a person finds themselves constantly feeling bad. If so, they can be helped to look at the way they perceive events to see if they would benefit from changing some of their thinking habits.

CBT attempts to alleviate depression by teaching techniques to correct the in-built negative distortions in the way events are interpreted. The therapist teaches individuals to look logically and rationally at the evidence for their views, and thus helps the depressed individual to adjust the way in which they see the world around them.

CBT can also be useful if an adolescent has experienced the highs of bipolar disorder. In this case it can provide techniques for coping with any fallout from the episode.

> I did cognitive behaviour therapy, which was just absolutely fantastic, it was really liberating, it stopped me from thinking in superlatives all the time, like 'I always make mistakes, I never do anything right, nobody understands me.' It stopped me thinking that way and got me thinking more realistically, like 'Sometimes I make mistakes and everybody does and that's okay.' So, it taught me to recognise my value and different ways of thinking because, from being ill for so many years, I'd learnt negative ways of thinking, and that taught me positive ways. **FJ, Bipolar Disorder Education Program, Black Dog Institute**

Interpersonal therapy

The onset of any depression occurs in a social or interpersonal context. Interpersonal therapy works on the premise that understanding the context can help the depressed person to identify it, master it, deal with it and prevent it recurring.

Interpersonal therapy makes no assumption about the origin of the depression, but uses the connection between the onset of the depressive symptoms and current interpersonal problems as a treatment focus. The therapy generally deals with current rather than past relationships, focusing on the immediate social context. It attempts to intervene in symptom formation and in the social dysfunction associated with depression, rather than aiming to change the more enduring aspects of personality.

Anger management

Anger is a complex and powerful emotion that can be tangled up with depression. It is also a common symptom experienced by those with bipolar disorder. It is difficult to deal effectively with anger, but necessary—neither quick release nor ignoring or forgetting such feelings is effective. Anger can arise from situations or life experiences that have caused disappointment, hurt or fear. It can also be in response to a violation of physical or psychological territory.

Adolescence can be a time of ready anger, partly due to mechanisms of self-control that are still maturing, and partly in response to the rather overwhelming changes that teenagers are experiencing. Those with depression or bipolar disorder may be particularly raw and have trouble keeping hold of their irritation levels.

Anger management can help a young person to master techniques for using the energy that the anger provides in constructive ways, rather than bottling it up, stewing and turning their anger inwards ('acting in'), or being hostile, volatile or irritable, or exploding ('acting out').

Other psychotherapies

There are multiple 'brands' of psychotherapy, each with varying emphases and approaches.

Many therapists tend to be empathic (good listeners), non-judgmental (trained to listen without feeling critical), and they do not dictate what people should do. The therapist's attitude is often one of unconditional positive regard for the client. They encourage a depressed person to 'ventilate' (talk about things that are concerning and preoccupying them).

The therapist may use the trusting and accepting relationship that grows between the individual and therapist (the therapeutic relationship) as a microcosm—a smaller, safer version of the outside world—so that interactions with the therapist can be used as a means of understanding the way the individual acts in real life. Therapy may be structured to a particular pattern or follow the priorities of either party.

Strategic therapies and counselling

There will be some therapies that are a better match to the teenager's type of depression. A talking therapy examining a person's reactions to life events will be of little use to a teen who is in the depths of a melancholic depression: they are unable to 'hear' until their depressive illness has lifted, which usually requires the assistance of medication. On the other hand, someone with a non-melancholic depression could benefit from CBT techniques, which could help them to manage and to shorten or even avoid further episodes of depression.

Direct counselling can often be of benefit to those with a personality style that has a leaning towards depression, or to the exuberance of bipolar disorder, helping them to mute their extremes of reaction.

THE BASICS OF A WELLBEING PLAN

A wellbeing plan reflects a 'stay well' emphasis that assists in bringing—and keeping—a mood disorder under control. Though professional support can help a teenager to start to overcome their mood disorder, keeping well and preventing further episodes usually requires an extra set of wellness strategies.

Remember, mood disorders can be recurrent, and vigilance is the price of mastery over them.

Draw on professional and other help

A wellbeing plan should be developed in concert with a practitioner trained in its nuances. Such a plan will include training in daily mood monitoring—for instance, completing a daily chart that quantifies mood swings, medication changes and stressors. It should also include the psychiatrist's or GP's advice about what extra medications the individual should take in certain circumstances (e.g. to promote sleep).

The wellbeing plan should nominate who the teenager will tell if they feel that they may be developing early warning signs of depression or a high, and it will formalise an agreement about *who* will take *what* action.

Also consider the option of support groups. There are groups for adolescents and also groups for carers.

It is wise to also nominate a person or persons who will provide 'outside insight' and whose role is to alert the teen to early warning signs that they may have missed if they have been swept quickly into the beginnings of a depression or a high.

Look at the triggers and early warning signs

The wellbeing plan will help the teenager to identify their early warning signs (e.g. sleep disruption, talking fast, spending excessively), and any triggers or stresses that appear to precede or prompt their episodes.

There are identifiable early warning signs for both depression and bipolar disorder. However, they may vary from episode to episode. For one adolescent, an early warning sign might be difficulty in getting to sleep at night because of worry; for another it might be muscle tension, headaches and loss of appetite; for a third, increased irritability. Becoming familiar with early warning signs and taking action when they occur is a vital part of preventing or softening relapse.

So, the wellbeing plan needs to list, if possible, the triggers and the early warning signs for that individual of an encroaching episode. For example, does their depression or bipolar mood swing follow on from periods of too little sleep, too much excitement, drinking too much alcohol, studying and working long hours, or not taking enough exercise? Once you have identified their triggers, you can help the young person to avoid them, and prevent or truncate further episodes.

Find ways to reduce stress

The wellbeing plan should develop strategies for reducing illness triggers and unnecessary stresses in the individual's life. For example, if a teenager's depression is caused by high levels of anxiety, unhelpful thinking and poor problem-solving skills, they may benefit from working on those issues with a mental health professional.

Understanding how a young person's personality works with particular kinds of stress means that you can help them tailor the management plan to their individual needs.

It is essential to modify the wellbeing plan to fit the teenager's circumstances, rather than hoping for the teen to fit the plan. If there is a setback, this may provide an opportunity to adapt the plan more accurately to the individual.

Overcoming hurdles provides evidence that they *can* be overcome. This may increase the teenager's sense of mastery and help them cope with any future difficulties or modifications.

STAYING WELL—TEENS SPEAK OUT

Wellness strategies help individuals to maintain their mental health and protect them from relapses. The following activities have proven helpful for many of our contributors:

- regular exercise—even if it's only getting off the bus at an earlier stop
- setting clear and achievable goals
- reading self-help and inspirational books
- using a mood diary to chart moods
- talking to friends
- listening to music (but not the heavy and dark varieties)
- writing in a personal journal
- scheduling regular enjoyable and rewarding activities
- reciting positive or inspirational self-affirmations
- rewarding themselves for daily achievements
- scheduling additional therapy sessions
- using meditation strategies to relax
- researching the internet for information
- humour: watching videos, looking at cartoons and reading books that make them laugh.

Some of these strategies are covered more fully in Appendix III, where we offer more reflections and experiences from teens on maintaining a sense of wellbeing.

Here is an account from a writer describing how her 'stay well plan' has reframed her illness for her. She is tolerant of occasional lapses in her self-management, but has become aware and mindful of her illness.

I think when people make a stay well plan they are aspiring to stay well, not to stay sick, and I think that's a really important distinction. And I also think that time makes a big difference. With knowledge, experience and time, people with mood disorders learn to control their symptoms and prevent relapses. So my advice to people who are still experiencing episodes of illness is to keep trying and keep trundling.

But it's often difficult to do all these things on a daily basis. I think there are times when it's okay to binge on junk food and choose not to exercise. The main point about stay well plans is that people with mood disorders move beyond the professional criteria and develop their own criteria for everyday life. To stay well, people are mindful of their disorder, even when they are symptom-free. I think this mindfulness—and this is the most important thing about stay well plans—gives you a sense of your personal strengths and your limitations. So, in making decisions about their everyday lives, people are taking into account the fact that they've got a chronic illness, and this awareness enables people to live well and prevent further episodes of illness. **FJ, Bipolar Disorder Education Program, Black Dog Institute**

Passing through the 'dark side' and mastering their mood disorder leaves many young people with a new sense of purpose, strongly inspiring them to reach out and help other people through those same shadows, as Brendan relates below.

Many people are left with a sense of 'mission' as they look back on their tussle with their mood disorder. Their aim is that, if there is anything that they can possibly contribute to prevent or soften the impact of an episode for another or to help someone who is making their way through the maze, then they will do it.

It's hard to know what I'm trying to get across here—I hope, however, that I can give someone, somewhere, some relief. In a way, I'd almost rather be telling this to just one person, because I want to change a human, not a bunch of statistics. I want to be reassured that I've done something, and that I've meant something.

When I think of who helped me out through this, it's just a blur. Whatever 'this' is, I'm still going through it. But I guess the difference is—no matter how hard it is—now I'm willing to try. As you may have noticed in my writing, I have an aversion to cliches, but I end up using them big-time anyway. I don't want to leave you with just a cliche. But if trying is a cliche then so be it, because that's all you can ever really do.

There are so many people I could mention here. And they help—if there's one thing I could say, it'd be that. But they can't do things for you, and that's what I'm trying to stress. If you're depressed, it's not your fault. If you can't fix it, that isn't either. But sometimes you can, and those are the moments you have to try and grasp at. **Brendan**

Here, another writer, Riley, shares the strategies he used to manage his depression and steer a new course to a sense of wellbeing. In it he emphasises the importance of recognising his own danger signs.

The first step on my recovery was recognition of a problem. There came a time when I felt that my life was a constant battle to get up in the morning, I was negative and unmotivated, sceptical of change. However, once people started to distance themselves from me I decided that I had a problem with depression. This led to the decision to change, a decision that could not be forced but was required for me to move forward. I found simply choosing to change frightening, as I was accustomed to the negative melancholy and felt almost secure in the depression. I was scared that change might make things worse, however I overcame this through positive self-talk which was basically a mantra: 'I am strong. I have faced danger and beaten it, I am fearless.' It was this mantra which I would repeat over and over whenever I felt scared or negative about changing my life, and this step in itself helped change my thinking from self-doubt to self-confidence.

In recognising the problem I found it was also important to believe that I could change my life around. At times I felt that all hope was lost and it was at these times I let the depression win, giving in to it and letting it control my life. When I believed I could make a difference in my life, however, I was able to change my thinking immediately and prevent a negative thought process from forming.

I then focused all my energy on changing my life around. I would work my frustration and anger out on a boxing bag. I also found that walking was a great time to get some space while being 'in the world' rather than hiding in my room. However, I did find my anger could lead to self-harm which, although I found it soothing, was potentially dangerous. I found myself thinking that if I couldn't change my life there was no point in living. I became determined to change and any time I encountered problems I would use the energy of the frustration to help overcome them.

Using anger is problematic at best, so I started using cognitive behaviour therapy (CBT): this is a process of positive self-talk to build self-confidence and replace negative, counterproductive thoughts. I found that the thoughts that I was using had to be believable—for example, 'I am able to overcome problems I encounter.' Self-talk such as 'I will encounter no problems, I will be fine' is unrealistic and can lead to feelings of inadequacy. I found the best CBT I could use focused on my positive attributes and I reassured myself that I had support and would make it through any problems that I experienced. Having friends that reaffirm your self-talk is very beneficial.

I found exercise was one of the key factors in coping with depression. Backed by science, it was recommended I started walking every day to ensure I get a natural boost of 'happy hormones'. A basic half-hour walk a day managed my stress levels, made me feel good about myself and helped with my depression. However, I found it incredibly difficult to motivate myself—the very nature of my depression was draining my energy and I just felt like sleeping. I then became negative about exercise, and more reclusive. This resulted in self-harm and counterproductive thinking. To counter this I needed to find the energy to use CBT (which takes a lot of energy to believe what you are telling yourself). The solution to this was I took time off from my studies and focused on healing my mind. However, it was my wanting to change that allowed me to do so. In retrospect I would strongly recommend sport to help with depression because it involves positive interaction, establishes a support network and you are able to use others as motivation.

The best approach to depression is one of understanding the nature of the beast: being able to identify when it is the depression that is making you feel like staying home, sleeping, et cetera, is crucial. And at these times I found if I did what the depression was preventing me from achieving I could loosen its grip on my life. However, to approach your life this way you have to *want* to change with all your heart.

I am now dealing with my depression far better than before, though there are still times when things become too much for me and my stress builds up. At these times I find it easy to become frustrated and angry, but this attitude is very counterproductive and can lead to depressive cycles. I found the best way to cope with a setback was to evaluate first how far I had come, accept that it was only a setback I was experiencing and not the end of the world, and then focus on positive self-talk.

I find it very useful also to have a list of strategies so when things become difficult I can quickly implement or reinforce a strategy that I know works. This quick recognition of a problem and decisive action to stop it prevents me from having any major setbacks.

Reclaiming your life from depression is a slow and painful journey, but with a strong mindset and a will to change, the only thing that will get in your way is your thinking. Be careful of negative thinking, and ensure you can recognise your danger signs. My danger signs are lack of motivation, anger and frustration, and negative self-talk. If you can identify your danger signs you can act.

Do not underestimate the power of the mind and the messages you give yourself! **Riley**

COMBATING STIGMA

Stigmatisation of people with mental illness is, unfortunately, still much in evidence. A very important part of the young person's adjustment to any disorder is the ability to handle discrimination as well as possible. Their resilience begins with their attitude to themselves, something that their caregivers also have an important role in shaping and nurturing.

One of the wonderful experiences for me, when living inside the dominant dark, fearful and destructive veil of a mental health problem, was the success stories my psychologist would provide. She would tell me about other young people who were of a similar age when they were sick, or who had similar symptoms. She would describe some of the issues relevant to their mental health and then tell me where they are today. I would hear from her about people she treated as children and adolescents; how they had completed high school, or gained employment, were in long-term relationships. I treasured these stories.

When I had the capacity to, I used such real-life stories to fight against the destructive forces inside my mind. I sincerely hope that in the future, publications featuring hundreds of these stories of young people's triumphs become available to primary school and high school students, in addition to being used within mental health services. **Lauren**

Our next writer, ultimately diagnosed in adulthood with a bipolar disorder, is very positive about her disorder. She has found that 'Education and information about the illness demystifies it, and allows those who have it to say, "I am a person who has an illness called a mood disorder", not the other way round.' She goes on to write:

I'd like to encourage people to be proud of who they are, encompassing their illness as well. And don't use stigmatising language about yourself, and educate other people to not do so as well. So, I'm Fiona and I have bipolar disorder, I'm not an illness, I'm not a 'manic depressive', I'm not a 'bipolar'. We are people that have illnesses. Person first, illness last.

So if you're a person with mental illness, don't be ashamed, and get as much education about it as you can and accept who you are completely. If you're a carer of somebody that has bipolar disorder, do the same thing: get as much education as you can, accept that this is a physical illness that manifests itself mentally, and do all that you can to take care of yourself as well.

And those of us who are both consumers and carers, we have a richness of knowledge to bring to our children so that they can learn to live life well despite having a mood disorder. It is a medical illness, nothing more, nothing less. **FJ, Bipolar Disorder Education Program, Black Dog Institute**

CARE FOR THE CAREGIVERS

Carers can face many challenges in caring for a person who has a mood disorder. These can parallel the issues faced by the person themselves, but they can also be different. Issues that have to be faced include accepting the diagnosis and learning how it's going to impact on your life.

Most importantly, to be the most help to the person you are caring for, you need to look after yourself as well.

It is important to be honest about any strain that you, as a carer, are feeling. A young person with a mood disorder may be unaware of the stress they are causing—if they are severely depressed or manic, it probably doesn't even register with them.

Because of issues of privacy and confidentiality, carers may feel unable to talk about the problems they are going through. It is comforting to have someone to talk to, to share the issues and find out how others are managing similar problems. Recharging your batteries can include joining a carer's support group, consulting a health professional yourself, or talking to a close friend or somebody else in the family about what's actually going on.

Coping with the unpredictable is a constant strain. Episodes of mood disorder and symptoms may differ each time. So, while the things you learnt during the young person's last episode will help, there may be other things you need to learn in this episode too.

As discussed earlier, it's essential to set some structures in place for times of emergency. Such an agreement should be put together while the teenager is well (if they have a relapsing condition). These agreements go by various names: Stay Well plans, Wellbeing Plans, Advance Directives, Ulysses agreements … What they have in common is that the young person and carer/s work out what is likely to happen, what the risks are, and figure out what they can actually do about it ahead of time. So, in the case of severe mood disturbance, this can include things like what hospital they are going to use, what medication they would agree to take, and what symptoms indicate that a mood swing is imminent.

Though it might seem difficult to cram even more into your already crowded week, add something for yourself—like exercise, tai chi, yoga, a massage, choir, quilting … whatever you enjoy. The renewed energy such outside involvement brings is immeasurable. It's enormously stressful looking after someone, and it really is important to replenish yourself.

The following are suggestions from Matthew and Ainsley Johnstone's *Living with a Black Dog*, mentioned in Chapter 7 —a book about how to take care of someone with depression while looking after yourself. Together with the teenager, and perhaps with the help of their counsellor, consider some rules that will help with overcoming stresses. Agree that:

- there is a situation that you are all facing together, so it is important to find the best ways of supporting each other
- you will fully support them, and they also need to help themselves
- you will all try to be as respectful of one another as possible
- everyone will try to communicate as openly and regularly as possible
- they need to follow the course suggested by their doctor and their counsellor
- you would like to talk with them regularly about how they feel things are going.

EDUCATION IS THE KEY

Many of our essayists were keen that preventive and early intervention strategies be implemented in schools and in families. A parent who reviewed the material in this book offered the following insight.

As parents, we don't just teach our children how to tie shoelaces and cut an orange, use good manners or budget with their pocket money, we also teach them (preferably at school) how to build a toolkit of coping mechanisms. Things happen which hurt us, which are unfair, which are embarrassing or frightening. If we do not know how to deal with these incidents—and especially if we have a personality style which predisposes us to an extreme response to these things—we are at risk of going on to develop a disorder.

Life's problems just keep on coming, we know that, but if we know how to deal with them we can move on. Strategies for coping are skills. They have to be taught. They are not necessarily acquired by enduring adverse events. Some people never learn them, and it is the role of parents and the education system to teach these in addition to the academic subjects. **Gabbi**

Another contributor outlines a range of ideas for improving the mental health of our young people.

Many suggestions for guiding children, teenagers and young adults through the maze of life forget one point that is imperative: adolescents need to be empowered and feel that their voices as individuals, as future adults, are heard. Solutions for adolescents will not be accepted if made by bureaucrats and politicians. Solutions such as: 'Conscription will sort them all out'—boot camps of indoctrination, juvenile detention or special hospitals for the hordes of mentally ill delinquents roaming the streets; or 'Full-time work will sort them out'. Or nostrums like: 'Whatever happened to all the good Christian families?', 'Why can't they just learn some self-control?', 'It wasn't like that in my day … We showed respect!' etc.

Some of the latest developments in programs that engage adolescents include initiatives that encourage collaborative effort—such as equine-assisted psychotherapy (EAP), where a relationship is established with the environment and a companion animal. Similarly, youth-focused programs that integrate living skills and nature workshops have been beneficial in addressing problematic behaviours in adolescents. These have included group and communal living in remote areas or wilderness settings.

Music therapies such as drumming and percussion workshops are also useful in engaging adolescents and instilling a sense of worth and achievement in completing tasks and acquiring skills. Music is one of the areas that generates interest amongst younger members of the community, and teaching music skills increases skills in other areas that include mathematics and basic numerical solutions, confidence, team-building skills and critical thinking. Learning the basics of a musical instrument is a process that emphasises dedication to a task, practice and memory. Drumming and percussion is particularly useful since it taps into primeval instincts that were accessed by our primitive ancestors during ceremonial worship worldwide. This may be a simple exploration of different sounds, beats and rhythms, or a structured program to learn the rudimentary principles of a specific musical instrument. Other instruments that are accessible and useful in this area are stringed instruments such as guitars, mandolins and basses. Brass and woodwind instruments are a little more complicated, however younger children are fascinated by the experience of blowing into a trumpet, for example, and making a sound.

Peer-education programs share an important role in dis-semination of information to adolescents who may experiment with alcohol and drugs. Teen camps that promote self-worth and address issues that are important to adolescents are also popular. In my day they were called 'sport and recreation' camps, and they gave parents an opportunity to send their children to a weekly program that included different sports, social activities and recreational activities such as sailing and boating. These camps were always characterised by bivouacs and songs around the campfire. Maybe it's just that parents need a rest from their children, and adolescents need a break from the 'oldies'. The generational space that is characterised by arguments, disagreements and open hostility is simply a human desire for freedom.

When we talk about 'grassroots solutions' for adolescent mood disorders, we often avoid simple approaches that may include wilderness adventure, nature walking, music therapy, art therapy or EAP. Why? What's the difficulty with promotion of simple solutions that engage human consciousness? What's wrong with educational processes that are not carried out in a classroom? **Lucien**

I think educating adolescents about mental health needs to be likened to sex education. Sex is not a seriously discussed topic among adolescent peers, or with parents, and mental health has a similar taboo. Based on my own experiences, I think there would have been great benefit in learning about mental health disorders in the context of health education. As with sex education, it would provide a non-threatening environment in which young people can learn to understand what it means to have a mental health disorder and how the mood disorders affecting many adolescents are very common in the wider community. As a teenager I remember thinking that depression was an illness in the same category as schizophrenia, and feared what might happen to me if anyone knew what thoughts were passing through my mind. **Xavier**

Health and emotional wellbeing strategies can be taught to young people regardless of their mental health status. In adolescence one can sometimes feel alienated and ignorant of the physical care needed to face life successfully. Learning skills such as cooking and meditation will have a positive outcome for a person's whole life, and the life of their children to come. Sometimes it is so obvious it seems to go without saying, because most people learn these skills as they go along. But if you've had an emotional upheaval, are estranged from family and friends and feeling down, it needs to be said. **Troy**

ARE THERE POSITIVES TO HAVING A MOOD DISORDER?

While it would be romanticising the issue to claim that people with a mood disorder would choose to keep it if they were given the choice, nevertheless many of the post-adolescent writers, looking back, say that reclaiming their mental health has given them an invaluable sense of themselves, and their mastery has also bred empathy, compassion and a keen desire to help others. While the lows may be frightful, and the highs damaging, charting a course through such choppy seas has left many people with surer instincts about their identity.

> I've learnt so many wonderful things from my illness. I've learnt compassion and passion and understanding. I've met so many wonderful people that I wouldn't have met without it. I've learnt to appreciate life, both because of the sadness, the depths of despair that I've been to with depression, but also because of my mania, and I've loved experiencing that as well. So I'm proud to be who I am today. **FJ, Bipolar Disorder Education Program, Black Dog Institute**

In her book *Night Falls Fast*, Kay Redfield Jamison observed that 'People seem to be able to bear or tolerate depression as long as there is the belief that things will improve'.[2] Here, to finish and to build on that observation, is an extract from the essay 'Grassroots'.

> At first there's the shock, fear, tears, recriminations and guilt around my brother's acute episode of mental illness. And then, after a very brief period of mourning for our 'old' lives, we are ready to mobilise. My parents arrange for my brother to see a psychiatrist, who diagnoses him and prescribes

antidepressants. The medication helps with the many physical symptoms of his depression. Mum then arranges for him to see a therapist, who finds ways for him to visualise and manage his stress, helping him regain control of his runaway thoughts and feelings. We all read as much as we can. Recognising that knowledge is power, we endeavour to familiarise ourselves with every warning sign and symptom, learning about the role of diet, sleep routines and exercise in keeping this menacing black dog at bay. Most of all, 'we' do this together, as a family.

In some ways the experience evolves from something stressful into something strangely positive and cathartic as we are all forced to stop and take stock of our busy lives. We come to appreciate the importance of taking time to be available—really available—to each other; to talk, to give hugs, to praise, to sit down to dinner together, to go on long walks in nature, to laugh, to cry and to take nothing for granted. My brother finds relief in that he is no longer hiding the darker part of himself from his family and has their unswerving support and acceptance. He works hard to coach himself to challenge his circular, negative thinking and comes to recognise that his thoughts are his own best protection rather than his worst enemy. Everything in our lives, from the grassroots upwards, begins a lengthy process of being overhauled, remodelled and reborn, and as a family we are all the better for it.

Two years later and Mum says she feels very proud to have such an emotionally attuned and deeply feeling young man as her son, and privileged to have been given an opportunity to come to really know him. He describes us as having 'caught him' when he was falling, and has since emerged as a gifted and talented educator of children. In this

> environment his sensitive soul and natural empathy is put to great use and he has flourished.
>
> Our family has travelled a dark and winding road, but together we have now arrived at a much happier and more hopeful place, where the sun shines most days and the grass is green and lush. The seasons may of course change and the grass develop occasional sere patches, but together we are no longer afraid of what tomorrow may hold; the roots that keep this family strong are deep and constant. **Amelia**

While this essay excerpt would seem to say it all, not all adolescents and families have such a positive outcome; for those who are still struggling, its sentiments could create irritation and even resentment.

We understand this reaction, however we suggest that the bottom line is generally an optimistic outcome. Mood disorders are being treated and brought under control more and more effectively—and with the adolescent's and family's resilience increased in consequence.

The key message is to give it time, for many management, self-management and subsequent adjustments need to be made. As the Argentinian author Jorge Luis Borges observed:

> Time is the substance I am made of. Time is the river that sweeps me along, but I am the river; it is a tiger that destroys me, but I am the tiger; it is a fire which consumes me, but I am the fire.[3]

Appendix I
Examining the use and effectiveness of antidepressants in teens

> The medication has also helped me. I have been on it for four months. I believe they have made me think before I react impulsively in bad situations. My mum was hesitant about me taking antidepressants as it is not recommended for under-18s, but she asked other doctors about it and supported my wish to give them a try. I don't know how long it will take me to get off these but in the future I would like to stop relying on them. **Rowan**

In the last few years, it has been increasingly suggested that some of the newer antidepressant medications intensify suicidality and violence—particularly in children and adolescents, for whom it is also held that such medications are less effective. Are such claims true or false?

BRIEF BACKGROUND ON ANTIDEPRESSANT TYPE AND USE

Generally, there are three broad classes of antidepressants.

The 'old' antidepressants—for example the tricyclic antidepressants (TCAs) and monoamine oxidase inhibitors (MAOIs) —are very effective in treating biological depressions, but may be associated with significant side-effects, need to be monitored carefully, and can be high risk if taken in excess. They are generally reserved nowadays for treatment-resistant biological depressions that have not improved with the newer antidepressants.

The 'old new' antidepressants—for example selective seratonin reuptake inhibitors (SSRIs) and selective noradrenaline reuptake inhibitors (SNRIs)—were initially thought to be as effective as the older antidepressants and blessed with fewer side-effects. The SSRIs appear to be less effective than the SNRIs—which in turn are less effective than the TCAs and MAOIs—in managing the biological depressive disorders. As we will address, they also have their own significant set of side-effects.

The 'newer new'—for example the noradrenergic and specific seratonergic antidepressants (NaSSA) and noradrenaline reuptake inhibitor (NaRI) antidepressants—were formulated as having a broader action, especially for the more biological depressive conditions—either when used alone, or in combination with other antidepressant medication classes.

If an antidepressant is needed for an adolescent with a non-melancholic disorder, then a narrow-action (i.e. targeting one neurochemical system) SSRI is usually the first choice, and rarely is there a need to progress to a broader-action antidepressant (i.e. targeting two or more neurochemical systems). However, for melancholic and psychotic depressive conditions, the SSRIs are often less effective than dual-action and even broader-action antidepressant medication strategies.

ADOPTION OF THE NEWER ANTIDEPRESSANTS

The advent of the SSRIs during the mid-1980s was hailed as a breakthrough: these medications were welcomed as having fewer side-effects, and clinically appeared to be not only as helpful as antidepressants for some types of depressive conditions, but also in their anxiety-reducing capacities. This means they can be of use in non-melancholic depressions when the adolescent has high trait (inborn) levels of anxiety, whether such anxiety is expressed as anxious worrying or irritability.

One major benefit of such antidepressant medications becoming mainstream was in helping to destigmatise the depressive and anxiety disorders. However, as with many 'miracle' drugs, some negatives emerged. Claims of the benefits of SSRIs were often exaggerated, and critics even then criticised their excessive prescription as an encouragement to 'cosmetic psychopharmacology'. Even the media fell in love with these medications. On the clinical front, the science suggested that, while up to 60 per cent of individuals were obtaining benefits, another 40 per cent were finding SSRIs ineffective or problematic. Side-effects were reported—sexual dysfunction for some, possible problems during pregnancy for the unborn baby, and serious problems with withdrawal ('discontinuation syndrome') if the medications were ceased too abruptly. For some, there was also a rare but dangerous side-effect on starting an SSRI—profound agitation. This was first reported in 1990, when six depressed patients developed 'intense, violent suicidal preoccupation' (akasthisia or agitation, sometimes called a 'serotonergic syndrome', which they described as feeling like they were 'jumping out of their skin') after two to seven weeks on an SSRI.[1]

Although the so-called SSRI or serotonergic syndrome is relatively rare (around 2%) it is a real risk, associated most particularly with serotonergic-based medications (such as the SSRIs). Competent clinicians now warn patients of this risk and suggest that if it occurs, the patient should stop the medication immediately. Many clinicians will also try to reduce the risk by starting at a lower dose than that recommended by the manufacturers. Clinical observation suggests that adolescents may be more at risk (around 5%) of developing such a reaction.

PROBLEMS WITH ANTIDEPRESSANT CLINICAL TRIAL PROCEDURES

There is a huge research trial literature out there, and the current evidence for the effectiveness of antidepressant medication in children and adolescents with depression is not very strong, with generally modest benefits (compared with placebo) being shown. As a result, many clinicians claim that antidepressants are ineffective and inappropriate in adolescents. However, in considering this issue there is a need to step back and examine the nature of the evidence base more widely.

We have argued[2] that there are major problems with the design of the randomised control trials (RCTs) intended to test the efficacy of antidepressants and psychotherapies. When weighing up research findings—and the meta-analyses that make up the evidence base—it must be remembered that the most severely depressed patients are usually excluded from clinical trials and this, and other methodological issues, limits the extent to which clinical trial data can be applied to a clinical population. Four broad areas of concern are now outlined below.

1. Selection of an unrepresentative sample

- Medication trial recruitment effectively excludes those who display: (i) psychosis, (ii) melancholia, (iii) excessive suicidality, (iv) bipolar disorder, (v) distinct co-occurring anxiety, (vi) failure to respond to adequate psychological management, and (vii) co-morbid organic and drug and alcohol problems. This means that the groups selected to test the effectiveness of antidepressant medications have been sanitised to the point where the participants do not resemble adults or adolescents seen in clinical practice.

- Recruitment is therefore skewed to uncomplicated 'reactive depression' conditions, and additionally biased to those patients who are highly likely to experience rapid response or spontaneous remission. For example, the placebo or spontaneous remission rate has increased at 8 per cent per decade—and it is currently not unusual for 60 per cent of such a selected group to respond to a placebo during a RCT.
- Volunteers for such studies are often financially reimbursed.
- Such recruits have a broad diagnosis of 'major depression' rather than being classified into depressive sub-types. If melancholic and non-melancholic depressive conditions are not sorted into separate groups, then their response to medication will be averaged across categorically different conditions, and the resulting response rate will be blurred. This approach means that treatments are tested as having universal rather than specific application, generating non-specific results.

2. Reporting biases

- Controlled trials may not ask about, measure or attribute certain side-effects.
- Following approval and release of medications, post-marketing surveillance may be limited.
- Medication-induced side-effects may be interpreted as due to depression (or the converse).

- Reporting tends to rely on doctors and is voluntary, as against reports from patients.

3. Publication biases

- There is a tendency for journals to publish only positive studies.
- Negative studies (i.e. where antidepressant treatment is not superior to placebo) are less likely to be submitted to journals, or published.

4. Interpretative biases

- RCTs are seen as able to generate definitive results (alone or via meta-analyses). This is wrong for, as detailed, conclusions based on unrepresentative samples contributing to RCTs do not resemble patients seen in clinical practice.
- Homogenising depressive sub-types into broader conditions such as 'major depression' makes it impossible to measure the effectiveness of any antidepressant medication, as it ignores the likely reality that some individual 'blended' disorders may be highly responsive and others quite unresponsive to the medication.
- Observers bring their own world views and biases (i.e. being for or against a particular drug treatment) when designing a trial and reporting its results.

ANTIDEPRESSANT EFFICACY IN ADOLESCENTS, BASED ON RCT 'EVIDENCE'

Studies have generally assumed that trials of the older broader-action tricyclic antidepressants (TCAs) in children and adolescents show no efficacy, and that trials of the newer antidepressants show slight superiority. Less commented on, however, is that trials of various evidence-supported psychotherapies also fail to differentiate from placebo. Such findings—based on group data—reflect the limitations noted previously.

It is also commonly assumed that the trials of antidepressants in children and adolescents somehow differ to those in adults, as the US Food and Drug Administration (FDA) doesn't release medications otherwise (though for licensing, the FDA only requires two positive studies—even if other studies are negative). However, when the trials are examined, there is in fact poor differentiation of response to antidepressant medications versus placebo across all age groups—that is, not just for children and adolescents, but for adults also. In the case of adolescent mood disorders, the task of selecting out which conditions are likely to benefit from such medication (and those who are unlikely to benefit) cannot currently be undertaken, as the grouped data do not allow such analyses and interpretations, again for reasons noted earlier.

THE RISKS FOR ADOLESCENTS

Whether adolescents are more likely than adults to develop suicidal (or akathisic) side-effects on the SSRIs is not yet known, but there are data from re-analysed trials that suggest that it is theoretically possible—the most common expression of depression in adolescence is irritability, so such a channel to agitation might be more easily activated in younger people.

Because their brain is not fully mature, adolescents are thus hypothesised as being at higher risk of:

- serotonergic (akathisic) reactions
- induced mania
- induced 'mixed' states.

While earlier studies[3] reported rates of suicidality and aggression in children and adolescents to be double in those receiving an SSRI or SNRI compared with those on placebo, subsequent studies researching this concerning issue have generated quite varying (both for and against) interpretations.

ADVERSE EVENTS WITH SSRIs

Our clinical experience suggests that, when initiating an antidepressant with an adult, there can be:

- severe to profound agitation in about 2 per cent of patients
- moderate and significant agitation in about 5 per cent
- psychotic features in 1 per cent or fewer.

However, as noted, the rates for these events appear somewhat higher in adolescents.

Further, when an antidepressant is abruptly ceased (or a dose is forgotten), there can be significant withdrawal effects in about 10–20 per cent of individuals. Such effects are not limited to SSRIs—they are seen in response to a number of the newer antidepressants—but these also appear more commonly in adolescents.

So, do antidepressants such as the SSRIs have a role in the treatment of adolescents? We would draw attention to the following points.

- SSRIs can be very helpful for some non-melancholic disorders, especially for people with an anxious worrying personality style that disposes them to depression. In certain circumstances (e.g. for the biological depressive disorders), SSRIs can be extremely beneficial and life saving. If they fail to assist an adolescent with a biological mood disorder, moving to a dual-action or broader-action antidepressant

medication class can again have major benefits.
- Such a cost–benefit issue is not unique to psychiatry or medicine.
- We argue that there should be a 'horses for courses' approach to treatment, as against viewing any antidepressant strategy (drug or non-drug) as having 'universal' application.
- Rather than RCTs, further clinical trials studying the effectiveness of antidepressants across differing depressive sub-types in real world clinical practice are needed.
- In 2004, the Treatment of Adolescents with Depression Study (TADS),[4] funded by the US National Institute of Mental Health, concluded that combination therapy (SSRI plus CBT) was superior to monotherapy (SSRI or CBT) for both impact on depression and in reducing suicidality. Such findings may argue the need for combination medication/ psychotherapy approaches, but may again be misleading if the studies combined individuals with differing mood disorder types.

WHAT DO THE DRUG REGULATION WATCHDOGS SAY?

Based on recent data analysis:

- The FDA in the United States and the UK-based Medicines and Healthcare Products Regulatory Agency determined that antidepressants slightly increase risk of suicidality (i.e. emergent or worsening suicidal thoughts and/or behaviours) in depressed children and adolescents. The UK has banned SSRIs for adolescent use, apart from fluoxetine.
- The Adverse Drug Reactions Advisory Committee (ADRAC), an Australian government body, issued a cautionary note in 2004 with a 'go ahead' to clinicians,

but only if antidepressants are used in conjunction with a comprehensive management plan.

WHAT NEEDS TO BE PUT IN PLACE?

- Clinicians and patients need to understand the risks relating to antidepressant use.
- Product information needs to be more explicit about worst-case scenarios for commencing and abruptly ceasing medications.
- Pharmaceutical companies need to monitor side-effects more closely during drug trials, and their surveillance systems for reporting such side-effects need to be improved.

IN SUMMARY

The non-specific nature of the efficacy results for antidepressants in adolescents does not clearly differ from the adult studies. This does not argue, per se, that antidepressants are ineffective, but more reflects the limitations of standard studies.

Currently, we do not know whether any antidepressant class (e.g. TCA, SSRI) is effective, ineffective or of comparable effectiveness in adolescents, because flaws in the modelling of the depressive disorders and the collection of the data obscures any answer.

Note this anomaly: only fluoxetine (of all the antidepressants) has received approval to be used to treat depression in people under eighteen years of age. Is this down to chance, or has it had more trials and thus FDA approval, or does this medication exert a real difference? On present clinical trial methodology, we are unable to say.

When a clinician plans a treatment strategy for an adolescent with depression, it must take into account:

- the severity and sub-type of depression
- the presence of co-morbid disorders and conditions
- the treatment history
- the adolescent's and parents' attitude towards treatment
- the presence of ongoing stressors.

Effective ongoing clinical management will then include continuing monitoring, educative and supportive psychosocial intervention, and techniques for managing daily problems.

THE POSITION OF THE RACGP

The Royal Australian College of General Practitioners (RACGP) guidelines on the use of antidepressant medications in children and adolescents are available at www.racgp.org.au. These guidelines were drawn up in response to an FDA report about adverse events in drug trials, where it was concluded that the risk of treatment-emergent suicidal thinking or behaviour was increased in both adult and younger patients taking an active drug (up to 4%) compared to those taking placebo (up to 2%), with the effect being more marked in depression than in anxiety disorders.

The management of severe mood disorders in children and adolescents, then, requires that the therapist weighs potential risks against potential benefits; notes current research findings; and monitors the clinical circumstances of the individual—particularly the emergence of suicidal ideation and behaviour.

Adolescents who are currently being treated for depression with an SSRI should not have their medication ceased abruptly.

When children and adolescents are commenced on an SSRI, the RACGP recommends:

- starting with a low dose and building up gradually
- warning parents and patients about potential activation symptoms, including the possible emergence of suicidal thoughts early in treatment
- careful monitoring in the early days and weeks for the emergence of behavioural activation, with the prescriber being available for contact
- consultation, wherever possible, with a child and adolescent psychiatrist
- seeing a developmental paediatrician in the case of non-response or significant deterioration
- following recovery, continuing the antidepressant for a period of six to twelve months to prevent relapse or recurrence.

The guidelines also state that tricyclics and MAOI anti-depressants have a generally higher risk of adverse effects, and much greater toxicity in overdose. Prescribing of these antidepressants for depression to children and adolescents should be initiated by a psychiatrist.

Medication is generally not recommended as a first-line treatment for children and adolescents with mild to moderate depression (usually a proxy term for a probable non-melancholic depression). In this less severely ill population, CBT or other appropriate psychological management is the treatment of choice. While the combination of SSRI medi-cation and CBT is held to be the most effective treatment for moderate to severe 'major depression' in adolescents, more definitive studies are required to test this proposition in adolescents with clearly defined biological depressive dis-orders such as melancholia.

CONCLUSIONS

The debate about the use of antidepressant medications in managing adolescent mood disorders has identified limitations to the science and to regulatory issues, and it has been muddied by other agendas. Currently, the focus on the risk side is wise, but this may mean that some adolescents who have biological mood disorders and who would benefit from an antidepressant may not receive such an intervention.

The prevailing media attitude probably relates to the initial oversell of the new antidepressants (i.e. that they were highly effective and without side-effects), with a subsequent loss of faith. However, the positive impact of these medications for many people—including adolescents—is rarely reported; the focus is currently overly weighted to negative issues.

More detail is provided in an excellent 2009 review by Vitiello.[5]

Appendix II
Assessing the risk of harm in teenagers with depression

The Beast may plague your thoughts and feelings but don't believe or act on them. Don't give up. There is hope. It will pass. You need to know what kind of a Beast you are dealing with.[1]

The message to teenagers who are at risk of self-harm is that feelings aren't facts, so don't act on them. A useful skill for a teenager to learn is to be able to stand back and disbelieve the evidence of their own senses and cultivate ways of cooling off, learning how to break out of an existing mind frame. These are skills best learnt and practised in the better times, and then employed in the worst times.

Some teenagers are at risk. Which ones? What are reliable indicators? Unfortunately, there are no dependable signs. The Australian Government Department of Health and Ageing website 'Living Is For Everyone' (LIFE) provides excellent information at www.livingisforeveryone.com.au.

Their research indicates that the potential for suicide and self-harm is determined by a mixture of family background, physiology, personality traits, emotional state, and family and social support systems. There are warning signs and tipping points, but these are not always obvious, and even skilled professionals can fail to detect them.

It is known that risk is heightened if the young person is left alone, has been affected (in particular) by alcohol, and has access to a ready means of self-harm. An adolescent may act impulsively in this state, and depression increases the risk.

> He knows the signs now. The first thought of killing himself and he knows he's got to get help. It's a paradox. He knows how worthless he is. How people loathe him and resent him. How pointless life is. He knows he should probably be dead. Yet he doesn't want to die. He doesn't want to abandon those people who say they still care.
>
> He can see the dangers in the way he's thinking, the way everything goes around in spirals; he hates himself and then hates himself more for hating himself. It cripples him because he thinks it's an indulgence and an imposition to voice his feelings. **Josh**

> I still bear the scars of the razor's edge, one of the many wounds encountered with countless 'dog fights' I've had over the years. The inner wounds are far uglier but, thankfully, no-one sees them but me. However, I am certain that all of you who have been bitten bear your own scars, seen and unseen. I know you can relate. Me writing this and you reading it undoubtedly proves one thing. We are fighters! We have already learnt or are willing to learn how to live with depression.[2]

The father of a teenage boy looks back on a very distressing time for his family. He calls his account 'Remember, Remember ...'.

Some events are so incredibly difficult to endure that they demand every single iota of concentration and strength available. Sometimes I felt that that last iota was being drawn from the tips of my toenails. After the event it is difficult to say what actually happened—so intense is the concentration and summoning of strength to go on.

Some events, however, will never be erased from my mind ...

My mind was racing with adrenaline. Silence filled the car. We were driving towards the hospital late at night. My thoughts were frantically speeding, 'Faster, faster' while an outward calm enveloped us all. Our thirteen-year-old son sat in the back seat. My mind was grappling: what could I possibly say? What did he need to hear? Surely some reassurance could be given, some comfort.

But what?

Into the thick silence I nudged the words, 'I can't imagine the incredible pain that you must be in to do that Sam.'

Affirmation.

Affirm his pain.

Silence.

The words settled.

'I'm guessing that you feel trapped, that there really is no end to it.'

The silence hummed with my wife's and my contemplation. I felt the deadness of thought from our son. I wanted him to know that we saw him where he was. I also wanted to give him some hope.

'Your pain will continue for a while yet, but one day it will be a lot easier.'

A stifled sob sounded from the back seat, and then another. Sam asked for the tissues. Then his hand crept onto my shoulder and remained there. My wife covered it with hers and thus they remained—tightly clasped until we reached the hospital.

During the course of the next three years our Sam continued to suffer from depression and 'chronic suicide ideation'. In 'parent language' that meant that somehow we had to convince Sam to stay with us in this world on a daily basis. *Every single day* we battled with Sam to show him that he did have a place in this society, that he did have something to offer, that life could be enjoyable one day, and that the struggle was worthwhile. While we were fighting with and for Sam, we were accompanying him to visits with GPs, psychologists and psychiatrists. We were sitting next to him listening as he answered questions with information that shocked us. That his little sister (then ten years old) had interrupted his first suicide attempt and had kept it secret— for six months ... That Sam thought about killing himself on a regular basis and would jump off the jetty where we lived—at low tide with weights fixed to his legs ... We were stunned at the original thought that had gone into his plans. Alongside these shocks were horrifying actions of self-harm. I screamed 'Nooo!!' in my soul to know of the arm peeled by the vegetable peeler, and the gushing of blood through cuttings—yet outwardly I remained calm and detached: 'Does that need stitches?' I was aware that Sam had great difficulty coping with *himself* and that he needed parents for stability and strength. I couldn't show the howling mess that I felt inside ...

Our family unit became tight and brittle.

Home was no longer a pleasant place to be. It was strained and tense. It was dominated by sadness, worry, fear, hopelessness, desperation, inadequacy (as parents), guilt and confusion. We all felt nauseous most of the time, my wife had difficulty keeping her mind on task to prepare a meal, and if she did succeed, no-one wanted to eat. Family members spent increasingly larger amounts of time in their own room. No-one had any news to share anymore; our whole life was centred on keeping Sam alive. The school rang us enquiring about the eleven-year-old—she was crying a lot at school. Even she—our usually bouncy, joyful child—was tense and teary.

We bought a TV. We had never had a TV as a family. We had put a high value on family life and conversing, reading, playing games, music and sharing one another's company. This had all disappeared and so we decided it was time to introduce TV! We not only bought a TV but we bought every funny DVD that we came across. We watched *Notting Hill*, *Two Weeks Notice*, the BBC *Coupling* series, *The Vicar of Dibley* series, Billy Connolly DVDs, and so on. We sat in front of the TV to eat our meals (a real break from our ideals of the past!) and we spent nearly all of our time together watching comedy TV. As we sat cuddled together we rarely laughed, but the TV comedy generated a more positive energy than we had experienced for some time. The eleven-year-old wanted continuous cuddles. She snuggled in and just wanted holding and loving. Sam too wanted frequent intense cuddles. (That broke my heart to have this tall lad clinging to me as if I were the last hope ...)

Then we bought a 'laughing bag'. We placed it in the lounge room and agreed as a family that every time any of us walked in or out of the room we had to squeeze the bag. It felt strange at first, but the silly sound of that bag laughing did help lift our mood.

We celebrated! We celebrated any tiny positive step. We celebrated that Sam had remained at school for an entire hour. We celebrated that Sam had come into a shop to buy some clothes. (My wife pre-arranged with the store manager that she would arrive at the least busy time and that he would serve us with his undivided attention.) We set up a celebration board with Sam and showed his accomplishments. His uncle (a pilot) flew in and 'collected' Sam to take him back to his family for a couple of days. We put a photo of Sam boarding the plane on the celebration board. Sam had to have an MRI. We put a photo of that on the board. We kept in front of Sam's face things that he had accomplished. We kept reminding him that he was achieving and moving forward.

We 'went into bat' for Sam. When we took him to family events we prepared the host in advance by saying, 'This will be really difficult for Sam to attend. We may leave after 30 minutes. If this is the case we would appreciate it if you would celebrate the fact that we have all managed to visit together for an entire 30 minutes rather than expressing disappointment at our early leaving.' Of course we had mixed responses, and some responses resulted in our non-attendance as a family.

Repeated lack of understanding of Sam's mental illness eroded the entire family's strength and confidence. My wife spoke about the situation on state radio and we established a support group for parents of adolescents. At the first meeting, my wife and I experienced a huge sense of relief. We were not alone and we were 'normal'. At that meeting and all the others that followed we discovered other parents in isolation, other parents lacking any support or understanding from those around them, deserted by 'friends' and judged harshly as a parent by relatives. The situations of those of us at the meetings were so similar we were amazed to discover the repetition of the stories. The parent support group became our monthly 'normaliser' and reassurer.

We became very isolated—apart from others we met along the 'mental health' pathway. At times the sense of isolation was so desolate and made us feel so friendless that we decided we must document those who were supports to us. When the days were tough and we couldn't think of a soul who understood or cared where we were, we could refer to our list that we had made in a more positive moment. My wife made a bowl out of clay and the family collected imprints of the hands of people who have supported Samuel and also us as a family, to fit into the bowl. This was placed in a stand—made by Sam—so that we could remind ourselves that we are not alone.

Sam is seventeen now—still with us, though still battling daily. We have been saddened to realise that understanding in the general community and even amongst so-called 'experts' is extremely limited. We sought assistance from professionals because we felt inadequate ourselves. We discovered that in many situations we had far more understanding and insight than the professionals we consulted, and that as parents we know a lot more than we gave ourselves credit for. Our greatest supports and strategies were those from each other. Our strength and defence came from insulating ourselves from the harsh judgments and criticisms of an ignorant community. Sometimes we just need to trust our own insights and realise that the greatest expert regarding any of our children is ourselves—the parents! **Connor**

THE RISK OF SELF-HARM

An individual with a mood disorder may find it difficult to keep pushing themselves along. The risk of self–harm can arise as:

- the direct result of the mental illness, and the thoughts and drives it engenders—which can sometimes be a wish to stop the pain, rather than necessarily kill oneself
- an outcome of reckless behaviour (e.g. speeding); self-harm and suicide are often associated with alcohol and other drugs—a so-called 'death wish'
- an attempt to end unmanageable psychological pain and despair
- an attempt to send a message, or gain an outcome such as notoriety, vengeance, defiance, or to leave a particular legacy
- an altruistic act, in the mistaken belief they are relieving others of a burden.

The risk is difficult to estimate as, for some individuals, self-harm can be impulsive and occur apparently without warning.

For the teenager who feels at risk of self-harm

If you feel at risk and unsafe, *tell* someone.

For carers

If there have been threats or changed behaviours, seek professional advice immediately. Some behaviours are more obviously high-risk—such as the teenager giving away possessions, or showing a sudden mood of relief, resolution and calm after a particularly bad patch—but remember that **there are no predictable signs**.

For professionals

Do not believe that entering into a contract—where the young person guarantees not to harm themselves—has any surety. **A contract does not provide any true guarantee of safety**.

Early warning signs of suicidality

These may include:

- expressing feelings of hopelessness and helplessness
- a drop in school performance
- painting, drawing or writing about suicide
- giving away personal possessions
- talking about suicide, saying things such as 'I wish I were dead' or 'What's the point of going on?'
- mentioning ways of killing themselves, and a plan
- talking about letting others down
- talking about feeling trapped
- leaving organised activities
- expressions of rage, anger, revenge
- abnormal sleep patterns
- dramatic changes in mood
- withdrawing from friends
- neglecting themselves
- engaging in risky, self-destructive behaviour
- sudden bouts of unexplained cheerfulness following a long period of sadness or anger.

These signs can vary across culture, age group and gender.

Self-harm triggers

Some things that can exacerbate the risk of self-harm include:

- recent life events such as a diagnosis of physical or mental illness
- the recent loss of a loved one or a pet, or the suicide of a friend or a role model
- a relationship breakdown or separation from a loved one

- a major disappointment, e.g. failing an exam
- involvement with intoxicants, particularly alcohol.

REDUCING THE RISK OF HARMFUL BEHAVIOURS

An all-encompassing and wide-ranging mix of strategies is needed to help safeguard young people at risk of self-harm. This could include measures such as:

- public awareness and training
- crisis and counselling services/centres
- school-based programs to improve resilience and coping skills, destigmatise mental illness, and build peer-based channels of communication
- stronger family ties, supportive family/friends, mentors
- sensitive, trained, available, professional carers
- coordinated and integrated care and service delivery
- screening for depression and suicide risk in schools
- building stronger social support networks in communities through sport and recreation clubs, etc.
- providing support for those bereaved, or with chronic or acute illness
- effective support, care and health environments
- a quick and sensitive response for teenagers in need
- follow-up after any crisis, and good continuity of care.

And finally, some words of encouragement and hope from one young woman who has made it back from the precipice and found a new inner strength.

> The scars that I have on my wrist from my failed suicide attempt are my visible physical reminders and sometimes when I start to feel the black dog approaching I look at these scars and remind myself of how far I've come. I'm not

ashamed of my scars or my past, nor am I ashamed that I suffer from depression. Today, I'm 23 years old and I work full time as a social worker. I've just completed my Masters of Social Work and for the most part I enjoy my life. My black dog still comes to visit me, the difference now is that I understand depression, although sometimes I deeply wish I didn't, and I know what I have to do to stop myself from spiralling out of control. I'm also fortunate that I know I can call on my old circle of strong women to help me through. But now, I've also started a new circle of strong women, of which I am a part. I'm not a hero, nor a saint, nor the great white hope. I'm telling my story not because I want to be any of these things, or to win a prize—that doesn't matter to me. I'm telling my story because, maybe, there is someone out there who needs it more than I do and who can draw strength and hope from it.

My black dog still visits me, but now I know I can face him and overcome his bites. **Tabitha**

Appendix III
Teenagers share their most effective wellbeing strategies

I'd like to talk about different 'wellness' strategies or ways of keeping well. Like treatment approaches, wellness strategies need to be tailored to each person's needs. One person might enjoy regular exercise as a strategy to prevent stresses from building up, while someone else might find a quiet hobby, or meditation, or reading more helpful for them.

In general, keeping well means taking care of your physical health by making sure that your diet, activity level and sleep are right for you. It can also be helpful to engage in activities you enjoy and that give you a sense of achievement: like making something with your hands or learning a new skill or a new language, for example.

FJ, Bipolar Disorder Education Program, Black Dog Institute

Here we cover in greater detail some of the strategies that teenagers themselves have found helpful in managing and alleviating their own mood disorder. A notable characteristic of the individuals who shared their tips is their fervent wish that what they have found effective for themselves might bring some comfort to others. Mastery of a mood disorder seems to breed, ultimately, generosity of spirit and a big heart.

Our next writer, now seventeen, has dealt with depression since he was eleven. He shares strategies that have worked for him, and what he's noticed along the way.

Talk about the mood disorder, seek help, and then modify your strategies:

- seek help from a specialist in mood disorders
- don't expect that psychologists etc. can 'fix' your depression: they can suggest solutions, but can't make you better
- talk to others with the problem and listen to their strategies. Then work out which of these strategies are relevant for you
- change them so that they fit with how you operate: big lifestyle changes are often too difficult to make because depression saps energy and motivation
- new strategies have to be built in slowly. For example (to increase the amount of exercise you get), if it's too difficult to go for a walk as an activity in itself, get off the bus a few stops early. The motivation and payoff is that you're heading for the haven of home.

Don't underestimate the power of the mood disorder:

- the paradox is that the first steps that can lead to recovery are those that the mood disorder prevents
- to overcome this, find a reason to fight, something that you enjoy, to gain a sense of achievement and some energy.

Take medication if relevant:

- While I need to take antidepressant medication, to take the edge off my distress, for me medication is not a cure, it's a crutch: on its own it is not a long-term solution. **Riley**

Rediscovering a passion can also open new doors.

I found I loved writing. My identity (my idea of myself) blossomed. Now I had highs I could trace and touch. I am not claiming I was 'cured' right away (writing brings fresh demons). And I am most definitely not claiming I have not struggled desperately at times. I am 35 years old and the truth is I will always be at war with the self-destructive side of myself. But it's a war I'm winning because I'm armed with love for the deed.

I suggest you:

- Arm yourself with your passion. Arm yourself with love for doing and learning.
- Tell somebody. Silence will lead you nowhere. Confiding in the right person in the right atmosphere will help loosen its grip on you. Give yourself and your listener faith and time.
- 'Travel' may be a daunting, even demoralising, word if you're living with bipolar or ongoing deep depression. Let me share something with you: you do not have to go to Egypt and redesign the pyramids. You can go a couple of hours away with a notebook, or sketchpad, or camera (or just yourself). Taking yourself somewhere different for a day is not beyond you. Okay, maybe not the best idea in your darkest or more chaotic hours, but most of the time. Needless to say, a road trip or train ride or long walk can't quash all sadness in your soul. But it

may defuse your thoughts for the day. You can come together with something indisputably bigger and more enduring—a stream or mountain or skyline or leafy road stretching somewhere.

- Remember how you loved riding or wandering somewhere as a kid? That feeling awaits you again. Can you picture any place it may be? Where did you last see it? There are other ways to get away, of course. Reading is a form of travel. It's an island, accessible all year, safe from the slings and arrows of emotional disarray and self-scorn. Provided, of course, you're prepared to do some burrowing for the stuff that's right for you. Writing, like music, comes in illimitable voices and shades. Join libraries. Raid your friends' bookcases. There are writers out there who will be as calming as your favourite musicians are uplifting.

- Sing. You may laugh or raise an eyebrow at that but I truly believe it will help you: I'd be pretending if I said I could explain it. Something to do with releasing pressure, I'm almost sure. When we live with depression and anxiety, we bottle up a lot of pressure. Unselfconscious harmonising and hollering is your birthright.

- You may have convinced yourself you don't have the creativity or dexterity for X or even-headedness for Y, but I'll bet you're an able, multi-hued figure. Maybe you've always wanted to be a more diverse cook? Or wondered how it feels to dance with a partner? Exploring life freshens and widens the reservoir from which your moods can be drawn. Weekly classes or short courses don't cost the earth. It's fun and healthy to meet kindred spirits. When I was younger I believed that I would only find out who I was ALONE. But it's with others we realise who we are, or wish to be. They show us—or suggest to us—how to live. In the right space at the right time, others inspire us. You can inspire those close to you by not giving up on yourself. **Ruby**

READ ABOUT MOOD DISORDERS

Read, read and then read some more. You and/or the teenager you care for can slip away to your local library if you need privacy, or if you'd like to browse the internet but haven't a computer at home. Some reading is helpful, some might better be avoided.

Here's an example where reading simply added to the confusion.

From learning of my mother's disconnection to reality [due to schizophrenia], I was consumed with what reality actually was. I phased into an existential period where I had so many questions of life. I tried to find answers by reading books that focused upon religion, philosophy and God; although I was never really satisfied. The hidden force behind many of my questions was the discomfort I could not break away from, that all my problems were beyond my control. It would make me tense all over to think that what I was feeling at the time, this severe hopelessness, would never go away. Life was so very complicated. I felt a sudden urgency about my emptiness. If I didn't fill it with something quick, I would become spiritually dead. I was extremely disappointed that I couldn't reason my way out of how I felt. **Daniel**

On a brighter note however:

Through research on the internet and books I would read in the corners of public libraries, I learned that depression was a real illness, affecting many more people than just me. This brought me a huge amount of comfort—just as reading stories of others living with depression did. It was around this time I felt empowered enough to try and change how I was feeling. I researched every alternative therapy to that of medication and then embarked on a crazy journey of supporting myself and my illness. I cast back to the years of being thirteen, fourteen and fifteen and have some fond memories. **Sarah**

ENCOURAGE THE TEEN TO TALK WITH SOMEONE THEY TRUST

Teenagers may find it hard to put their feelings into words. If this is the case, they can at least talk about how their feelings have affected their behaviour—for instance, the activities that they no longer can do or enjoy.

It was not until I was sixteen that I spoke to anyone about how I felt. And this is when things really did begin to change. I had spent so much time pretending to everybody who knew me that I was a 'normal happy-go-lucky teenager'. I had tried to stop my tears and dark thoughts all by myself and it was just not working.

I remember the day I talked to my mum about how I was feeling. We were in the car, parked near a park where my little brother was playing. I started to shake and cry and actually did not have to say anything. Mum turned to me and said, 'You have not been feeling okay for a long time, have you?' We talked about depression and she told me how prominent and common it was in both her family and my dad's family. The pressure which was lifted off me that day was just unbelievable. How I had been feeling was validated and I no longer felt I was abnormal or weird or a freak who had to hide myself away. **Sarah**

I was periodically late for my Thursday maths class with Ms Krueger; sleeping in became something of a habit. Ms Krueger saw not only my lateness, but also the drop in my results and the bleak disinterest in my attitude as a clear sign. She recommended that I talk to the school counsellor, Brian. She said that it was entirely my choice and I could quit at any time, only that I see him. I was initially resistant to the idea but eventually accepted the one session. It would come to be, throughout the entire year, a total of nine sessions with him.

Counselling immeasurably helped me. Brian didn't know me and that was important. I was able to say a lot of things to him which I couldn't with anyone else. And for all my puzzling questions on life, he would ask several more and either cast doubt on whether the questions themselves had meaning or if it was the right question to be asked. It didn't bother me that he couldn't answer them. He never dismissed what my own opinion of them was, and that actually meant a lot to me.

Brian expressed the immediate positives in my life that I was blind to and motivated me to try again at life. I felt a renewed sense of self during those sessions. **Daniel**

GET THE TEENAGER TO WRITE IT DOWN

Many people find it helpful to write down their experiences—both pleasant and unpleasant. Writing can 'track' moods; anchor the individual; confirm that previous low moods have passed, and what they were associated with; and recall the better times during a stage when the teen is feeling low.

It can also help the teen notice when another episode might be sliding in. Such advance 'weather forecasting' is valuable in that it enables early intervention, and gives you and the young person some time to bring into play psychological tools/approaches—including increasing medication dosage, if that is relevant.

> Writing became my only way of releasing the demons inside; at times it was a chaotic scrawl of words on a page, other times it was neat and methodical—my writing style echoing the two sides of me. I could write for hours in a therapeutic yet hostile state of release. A downside was that I became so reliant on my journals that I probably somehow lost the ability and courage to talk to others about what I was experiencing. **Jessie**

HELP THE TEENAGER TO CULTIVATE FRIENDSHIP

Friendship is a great solace—provided it is with someone a teenager can trust. Adolescence can be a time of shifting loyalties, so hopefully the young person can be helped to seek out a person or group that feels 'kindred' to them and seems aware of what they are feeling. It is important, however, for them not to overly burden friends with their distress: friends are not a substitute for professional help.

> My greatest freedom and shift in myself was just around the corner and it came in the form of a new friend: a living, breathing person. Someone who had been through similar and had come out the other end, she was slightly worse for wear but she was okay. I had lots of friends, but none that I could connect with anymore. I just felt like I was in a glass jar and could see the world outside but

couldn't touch it—all my old friends and family were still there but I just couldn't touch them anymore. Having a friendship and an environment where I could be myself without having to hide anything, and more importantly without having to explain anything, was a godsend. That friendship saved my life. It allowed me to breathe while I adjusted and learned to manage my depression and anxiety.

I went on to find a great counsellor, someone who I felt really comfortable with, and together we worked through some of the baggage that had contributed to my meltdown. I think the most important factor for me, and one that has proved the biggest challenge, was to establish a reliable and healthy support system. A full-time one, places I can go to or people I can be with that are healthy and supportive and stable. A support system that helps me 'enable' myself. For a long time I looked to professionals for someone or something to 'fix' me. But I realised that in the end I am the only one who can make any real changes and that I was the captain of my own ship. **Luke**

HELP THE YOUNG PERSON TO SORT THOUGHTS FROM FEELINGS

It is very important to try to reinforce the difference between facts and feelings. Feelings aren't facts, so they shouldn't be acted on. Negative emotions alert us to problems, whether they are real or imaginary—but strong feelings can have a downside. An 'emotion storm' may sweep through a young person and convince them that this is the way the 'weather' is permanently. Get them to remember climate change—in the best sense of the term.

Feelings can be differentiated from thoughts by putting 'I feel …' or 'I think …' at the beginning of a response to a proposition or question. Getting the teen to know his or her feelings can help them gain access to a broader and less intense set of reactions. If the young person can just stop for a minute in order to assess their feelings in a particular situation, this can give them an edge, better control, better perspective, and fewer reasons for regret.

The next extract illustrates—with humour—the capacity of poorly understood waves of feeling to destabilise an individual. The writer might have found it helpful to sort things through with a counsellor, and maybe to have learnt some strategies from a cognitive behaviour therapy (CBT) approach.

When news came that Jackie was engaged, the blow sent me reeling in convulsive tears. How unbelievable it was that colourless Jackie had scored herself a permanent man! This left only me from our schoolgirl group unaccounted for, I alone had been unable to secure someone to love me. The humiliation could scarcely be borne. I was already past my nineteenth birthday and had been left behind: my mother's warnings to my ten-year-old self, that nobody would ever find me lovable, had come to pass. The prospect of pressing on through another nineteen years as empty as those already lived could not now—now that even the nonentity Jackie was engaged—be contemplated. I must die today, die right now, and by suddenly dying, escape the scorn that my singleness would evoke at the weekend, when, if I was still alive, I would have to attend the Christmas party alone and clearly loveless. **Lucy**

HELP THE TEENAGER FIND SOMETHING THEY'RE GOOD AT

Down moods can bring teens to a standstill. If the young person is stuck, stale, or finding school and/or friends impossible, kick out into something new.

Help them to join an art class, creative writing, a sewing course, select a penfriend, learn a musical instrument, do something challenging like a public speaking course, become a bit of an expert at a computer application—graphics, or desktop design. The local library or the internet has a host of further suggestions. This may seem vapid in the face of the teen's present distress, but stages of recovery can leave room for some slight interest which may grow and help access new energy and direction.

One thing that might seem slight, but was an incredible comfort to me at that time, was my interests. The monster in my head had pretty much eaten everything I liked right then—my drawings were sloppy and impatient, my writing and words had dried up, philosophy scared me too much and the thought of attending karate again sent me into a panic attack—but I wanted something. I have always been a very self-absorbed person, not in an egotistical jerk sort of a way—hopefully—but very introverted, and constantly analysing myself. At this point, I needed to talk about myself, to confide in someone, and that's when I went looking for those people. I turned to the internet, which I, by that time, was spending hours each day on, and found several pen pals. **Brendan**

TEACH THEM TO REMEMBER: 'IT WILL PASS'

Console the young person with the knowledge that this episode—this mood swing—will pass. The teenager can track their moods by keeping a journal, and in bleak times read over passages in which they have noted the lifting of previous down moods. Another thing that some people find helpful is a box with a collection of items that they treasure. The postcards, letters, prizes, recognition, mementos of celebrations and photographs can all be a reminder of sunnier times.

When I get really low I try to have faith, I remind myself that my mood will lift again like it has before. I look at old photos and I listen to my favourite music. Even though I can't remember how I felt when I didn't feel so dark, I know that I did feel differently. Music has always been a big helper, and listening to radio programs on the more with-it stations.

I try not to watch too much television—I find all the advertisements and clips of crime shows and the news distressing. I'm generally not even aware that they 'get' to me until after I turn them off and can notice the residual tension.

Somewhere amongst it all I plumb myself and find the strength to ride out my bleak days, to go to sleep at night and to wake up and face the next day. As I trudge through, I remind myself that each day brings new opportunity and new possibility, and is one day closer to a good time again. Sometimes it's hard not to give in and give up. The thoughts are so dark and they swallow everything, but I know I have pulled through this before and I know so many others have made it through as well. And when life is good I'm always thankful that I hold on during those dark moments, even if it is only just by a thread sometimes. **Luke**

Appendix IV
The Mood Assessment Program (MAP)

The MAP, a world-first assessment and diagnostic program for depression and bipolar disorder, applies the logic detailed in this book, and may therefore be worth considering. While designed for completion by adults, pilot testing indicates that it is likely to be of assistance to adolescents aged sixteen or older.

INTRODUCTION AND HISTORY

The MAP is a computerised assessment and diagnostic tool which incorporates the know-how of experienced mood-disorder specialists, and can provide clinicians with diagnostic and management advice to assist people with mood disorders (both depressive and bipolar). Just as an X-ray or a pathology test can provide medical practitioners with additional diagnostic information, the MAP can provide clinicians with both general and specific information about the mood disorder sub-type, factors contributing to the condition, and broad management options.

Professor Gordon Parker commenced development of the MAP in 2002. Subsequent development and pilot studies have been funded by NSW Health and the Black Dog Institute.

The MAP has been used by hundreds of health practitioners across rural and urban New South Wales, Australia. It is delivered over the internet, providing convenient access for people regardless of their location. Health practitioners provide people with a special MAP access code, which allows them to complete the assessment at home, or within the health practitioner's rooms. It is very easy to use, even for people who have never used a computer before.

Data from the assessment is securely transferred to the Black Dog Institute where the MAP system runs a set of diagnostic algorithms to generate a comprehensive MAP Report. This report is immediately sent to the referring health practitioner via secure clinical systems, or a paper version is mailed to the referring health practitioner the next working day.

The report contains a wealth of information including important diagnostic probability decisions. For example, does the person have unipolar depression or a bipolar disorder, and is the depression a melancholic or non-melancholic depression? Lifetime and current anxiety disorders (conditions that commonly drive secondary depression) are screened and recorded. Depression severity and clinical features are identified. Previous treatments (and their helpfulness and/or cessation because of side-effects) are recorded in the report, as are risk factors, at-risk family history and developmental features. The report finishes with a set of treatment suggestions to assist the referring health practitioner with further management. The information is presented in a format that can be readily used by the health practitioner in preparing a management plan specific to individual patients.

For further information about the MAP, contact the MAP team at the Black Dog Institute. See www. blackdoginstitute.org.au.

Glossary

Acute: Refers to the rapid and recent onset of an illness—one which is commonly severe and intense. An acute illness might improve, or proceed to a more chronic state.

Adverse event: Any unexpected medical problem that happens during treatment with a medication or other therapy.

Affective disorder/illness: One in which a mood disturbance is the primary or defining characteristic, such as depression or bipolar disorder. A person with depression experiences a persisting very low mood, whereas a person with bipolar disorder is hampered by both very low and very elevated mood states.

Akathisia: Essentially a state of motor restlessness that is most commonly a side-effect of antipsychotic drugs but which can have other causes, including being a side-effect of antidepressant drugs.

Antimanic medication: Medication supplied to help stabilise the highs of bipolar disorder.

Antipsychotic medication: Medication supplied to prevent or soften a psychotic episode, but which these days can also be used to settle a manic high. It can also be added to an antidepressant (as an 'augmentor') to promote its antidepressant action.

Augmentation: Medication augmentation increases the effectiveness of one medication by adding another from a

213

differing medication class. (Combination therapy involves two or more medications from the same class.)

'Bipolar' or bipolar disorder: Once called manic depressive illness, bipolar disorder refers to an affective disorder characterised by episodes of mania (highs) or hypomania alone, or with depressive episodes (lows) at other times. It is now subdivided into two main types: Bipolar I and Bipolar II (see below).

Bipolar I: This involves episodes of mania and depression. The highs are generally more severe and last longer than those in Bipolar II, and may be associated with delusions and/or hallucinations.

Bipolar II: This involves episodes of both hypomania and depression, but no experience of mania.

Bipolar depression: An episode of depression in a person with bipolar disorder. The depression is severe, and almost invariably melancholic or psychotic in its expression.

Chronic: When an illness (or stressor) has continued for a long time.

Circadian rhythm: Humans, like all living things, have a body clock—an internal biological setting that regulates our functioning. The body's circadian rhythm is one of the first systems disrupted in a mood swing. As well as daily rhythms there are larger yearly patterns, with some people particularly vulnerable to mood swings at the change of seasons. Intervention to normalise the sleep–wake cycle is often helpful—as is avoiding situations that disrupt this cycle, such as flying across time zones, and shift work.

'Client': See 'consumer'.

Clinical depression: An episode of depression that has been present for most of the day for two weeks or more, is severe in its expression, and is associated with impaired functioning (at home or at work).

Cognitive behaviour therapy (CBT): CBT is a psychotherapy that attempts to alleviate depression by providing tools to help examine the truth of everyday assumptions and interpretations, as some people with depression often have a negative view of themselves (even when not depressed), and develop thinking patterns that are so habitual that they don't notice their irrational judgment.

Compliance: Following the treatment instructions of the health professional with regard to medication and other interventions. It is synonymous with the term 'adherence'.

'Consumer': The terms 'client' and 'consumer' are used by those involved in mental health to refer to a person who has used or is currently using mental health services. The intent is to empower people, rather than calling them 'patients'.

Counselling: Counselling involves listening, empathy and helping the client to structure and make sense of their experience. Finding solutions to personal problems can be of benefit to those with a personality style that has a leaning towards depression. Counselling may be provided as a part of other strategies, or as the sole therapeutic approach.

Delusional depression: This is also known as psychotic depression. The person experiences false beliefs (delusions) during a depressive episode, and/or false perceptions (hallucinations).

Depression: A broad term that can encompass normal mood states, clinical syndromes and actual disease states (e.g. melancholia). At the 'clinical depression' level, it involves body, mood and thoughts, and affects a person's view of themselves. Symptoms include loss of interest and pleasure; loss of appetite, with weight loss or weight gain; loss of emotional expression; a persistently sad, anxious or empty mood; feelings of hopelessness, pessimism, guilt, worthlessness or helplessness; social withdrawal; and unusual fatigue and low energy.

A depressive disorder is not the same as a passing 'blue mood' or transient sadness. It is not a sign of personal weakness, or a condition that can be wished away. Without treatment, symptoms can last for weeks, months or years. Appropriate treatment, however, can help most people with depression.

Differential diagnosis: Accurate diagnosis requires careful consideration of possible alternate psychiatric and medical disorders that may have similar symptoms. Doctors will frequently give a preferred diagnosis (the provisional diagnosis) for the present, but consider or list one or more differential or alternate diagnoses to keep in mind if there is ambiguity.

Diurnal variation: This is a change in depressive mood and energy level at certain times of the day. In general, those with melancholic depression report that their mood and energy is worse in the morning; those with non-melancholic depression describe the opposite. People with psychotic depression report no diurnal variation.

Drug (medication) classes: Medications can be divided into different 'families' or 'classes' of drugs on the basis of their chemical backgrounds. Drugs from within the same class or family have a similar chemical makeup.

Dysregulation: Mood dysregulation is when severe mood swings occur that are at the extreme of the normal range— the moods are either too intense, or lacking intensity.

Electroconvulsive therapy (ECT): A modern psychiatric treatment that is effective across a narrow range of psychiatric disorders, including melancholic and psychotic depression. It is occasionally also used in the treatment of manic disorders and certain types of schizophrenia. It has been established as the most effective antidepressant treatment available for melancholic and psychotic depression, and is a therapeutic option if other, usually beneficial treatments for those conditions have been unsuccessful. Research has shown that more than 80 per cent of patients who have had ECT are willing to receive the treatment again.

Endogenous depression: An older term for melancholic depression, reflecting the view that such depression was not related to stress but arose more from within the individual. Present evidence argues for rejecting this term—as most depressive sub-types are preceded by stressors.

Episode: This refers to a bout of illness, whether mental or physical.

Formulation: This is not synonymous with diagnosis but seeks to explain the dynamic and multiple factors that have resulted in the individual developing a condition at that particular time.

General practitioner (GP): A medical doctor who provides general all-round care. A GP treats acute and chronic illnesses, and provides preventive care and health education for people of all age groups.

High: A term used for the abnormal upswing in mood that is characteristic of hypomania or mania.

Hypervigilance: An anxiety state of being too 'switched on'. The person is abnormally watchful and on guard all the time, scanning their surroundings for 'threats', being easily startled and over-reacting.

Hypomania: A high that is less severe than the highs of a manic episode, and without any psychotic features.

Interpersonal therapy: A time-limited treatment for major depression. It uses the connection between onset of depressive symptoms and current interpersonal problems as a treatment focus, generally dealing with current rather than past relationships, and focusing on the immediate social context—particularly role changes in dealing with work and relationships.

Introjection: When a person's sense of themself and/or their attitudes and opinions is built from the views of others. The person incorporates or takes in these views and believes that these views are their own.

Kindling: This is the name for the effect observed when an affective illness starts out as occurring only in response to stressors, and then progressively takes on a life of its own—with episodes often emerging without any preceding clear stressor. The brain is a highly regulated system with a lot of feedback loops, and if it is stressed, then rested, then stressed again repeatedly, it can become increasingly sensitised to such stress; the reverse of 'tolerance'.

Maintenance therapy: Therapies (usually medication therapies) that are either in place, or are put into place, after the individual's episode has been brought under control. Maintenance therapies are designed to keep the person well and prevent the onset of a new episode.

'Major' depression: A broad diagnostic term describing an episode of depression with five or more specific features (e.g. depressed mood, loss of interest and pleasure, sleep disturbance) that is present for two weeks or more, and associated with social impairment.

Mania: An observable high mood in which a person is often psychotic (has lost touch with reality) and is experiencing delusions and hallucinations.

Melancholia/melancholic depression: A 'biological' type of depression that is likely to emerge without any obvious stressors involved. It has a genetic basis, and distinct clinical features such as slowed movement and non-reactive mood. It generally responds to medications, but sometimes ECT is a necessary treatment.

Meta-analyses: Essentially involve analyses of aggregated data from multiple individual studies, principally to benefit from a large database and overcome idiosyncratic results from individual studies.

Mood: This is a personal description of how an individual feels (contrasting with 'affect', or how the individual appears). It can also be a persistent emotional state.

Mood disorder (or 'affective disorder'): A mental health problem characterised by distortion of mood—the profound sadness or apathy of depression, the euphoria and highs of bipolar disorder, or swings from one to the other.

Mood stabilisers: Medications that help to control the fluctuations of mood (i.e. highs and lows) that typify bipolar disorder.

Neurotic depression: A dated term used to describe a depressive sub-type in individuals with particular personality styles (such as neurotic, highly anxious, shy and unassertive) that were thought to dispose them to greater risk of depression when faced with stressors.

Overvalued ideas: These differ from normal thoughts in that their presence is encompassing and preoccupying, and in the intense and fixed way that a person holds to them. In practice, they appear somewhat 'abnormal', but they are not extreme enough to be psychotic.

Pharmacotherapy: Another term for medication therapy.

Physical treatment: A term used for a treatment (e.g. medication or ECT) that is designed to modify biological processes, as opposed to psychological interventions.

Placebo: A placebo is a neutral substance used in controlled experiments to test the effectiveness of a medication and to provide a basis for comparison of effects. Ideally, it should be indistinguishable from the active drug being tested. In the study, one group will be given the placebo, while another will receive the agent under evaluation. Neither group will know whether they are receiving the active drug or the placebo. (In an interesting phenomenon, placebos have been shown to actually lessen symptoms in some people, most likely because they have positive expectations about any treatment interventions.)

Primary depression: This means that the depression is a person's main or sole condition; it 'stands alone'.

Prophylactic medication: This is medication prescribed as a preventive measure to stop a disorder from occurring or recurring, even though the disorder is not currently active. The term comes from a Greek word meaning 'an advance guard'.

Provisional diagnosis: This is the interim diagnosis that is made by the clinician until other factors clarify and confirm the disorder. A provisional diagnosis is usually listed together with the 'differential' diagnosis that lists other possible disorders in order of likelihood.

Psychopharmacology: The science of drug therapy for psychiatric disorders.

Psychosis: Impairment of mental functioning in which the individual loses touch with reality and usually experiences delusions and/or hallucinations.

Psychotherapy: This is a non-physical treatment in which the therapist adopts a particular approach (e.g. analytic, interpersonal, cognitive, cognitive-behavioural) to address symptoms and/or personality problems experienced by an individual. It involves a number of non-specific components (e.g. empathy) that make a therapeutic contribution.

Psychotic depression: Severe depression with the added presence of psychotic symptoms—that is, delusions and hallucinations.

Randomised control trials (RCTs): Assess the efficacy of a drug or non-drug treatment in comparison to a placebo (inert substance) or another active treatment or 'comparator'.

Rational emotive therapy: This was developed by the American psychologist Albert Ellis, and was a forerunner of cognitive behaviour therapy.

Reactive depression: This is an outdated term for a depressive episode that can be explained as a consequence of having experienced a major stress.

Recovery: When a depressive episode has completely resolved for a defined period.

Recurrence: A new episode of depression, after an individual has been completely well from depression for a defined period.

Relapse: The return of a full episode of depression, when the individual has not completely recovered from an earlier episode.

Remission: When an episode of depression (or mania) has resolved completely, but the period has been so brief that it is not clear whether actual recovery has occurred.

Schizophrenia: A psychiatric condition where delusions and hallucinations are common, thinking, insight and attention are often impaired, and there are frequent behavioural problems. It is quite distinct from the mood disorders, although a significant percentage of people with schizophrenia develop a superimposed depression.

Seasonal affective disorder (SAD): This is the name for the depressive episodes that can occur on a reasonably regular basis in certain seasons (especially autumn and winter), and resolve in the alternate seasons (spring and summer). The clinical feature pattern may differ from classic depression. Phototherapy (bright light therapy) may be effective. Also see 'Circadian rhythm'.

Secondary depression: This type of depression follows, or is otherwise related to, another major medical condition, whether psychiatric (e.g. anxiety disorder), medical (e.g. a stroke), or another factor (e.g. alcohol abuse).

Self-esteem: Also known as self-worth or self-regard, self-esteem is related to how we view ourselves. Those with positive self-esteem regard themselves as worthwhile and valuable. Those with negative self-esteem feel worthless and useless. Low self-esteem used to be known as having an 'inferiority complex'.

Side-effects: Unintended effects of a medication that can exist alongside any of its positive effects. Side-effects are usually most pronounced in the first few weeks of treatment, but others (e.g. weight gain, thyroid dysfunction) may appear only after more prolonged use.

Somatic: To do with the body—for example, a somatic (physical) illness.

Stigma: A sense of shame felt by people with a mental illness as they try to go about their lives in the face of discrimination by the wider community.

Stressor: An event or interpersonal interaction that causes distress. Stressors can be acute (e.g. the immediate aftermath of an accident), or chronic (e.g. poverty, a poor marriage).

Titration: When used in reference to a medication, this term means adjusting the drug to the most effective dose for an individual.

Trait: A genetically based ongoing feature, such as personality style.

Unipolar depression: In contrast to bipolar depression, this is a term originally used to sub-classify the behaviour pattern of people with melancholic depression who experienced only depressive episodes. It is now used to describe the course of any non-bipolar condition.

Wellbeing plan: For those with a mood disorder, such a plan is designed to provide self-management strategies for reducing the chance of episodes and for managing mood episodes. Components include mood charting, identifying triggers, removal of stimulants (e.g. drugs, alcohol), de-stressing activities (e.g. meditation), and agreed-on 'action plans' with relatives or friends if an episode occurs.

Notes

PREFACE

1   T. Wigney, K. Eyers and G. Parker (eds), *Journeys with the Black Dog: Inspirational stories of bringing depression to heel*, Allen & Unwin, Sydney, 2007. K. Eyers and G. Parker, *Mastering Bipolar Disorder: An insider's guide to managing mood swings and finding balance*, Allen & Unwin, Sydney, 2008.

CHAPTER 1

1   J. Godfrey Saxe, 'The Blind Men and the Elephant', www.noogenesis. com/pineapple/blind_men_elephant.html [24 March 2009].

CHAPTER 2

1   From T. Womersley, 'Burden of new manhood leads to depressing rise of the Atlas syndrome', *The Scotsman*, 25 August 2003.
2   M.G. Sawyer et al., *The Mental Health of Young People in Australia: The Child and Adolescent Component of the National Survey of Mental Health and Well-being*, Commonwealth Department of Health and Aged Care, Canberra, 2000.
3   S.R. Zubrick et al., 'Mental health disorders in children and young people: scope, cause and prevention', *Australian and New Zealand Journal of Psychiatry*, vol. 34, 2000, pp. 570–8.
4   Australian Bureau of Statistics, *Child and Adolescent Component of the National Survey of Mental Health and Well-being*, Canberra, Australian Government Publishing Service, 1997.
5   M. Carr-Gregg, *Surviving Adolescents: The must-have manual for all parents*, Penguin Books, Melbourne, 2005.

CHAPTER 3

1   M. Greenberg, *Hurry Down Sunshine*, Random House, New York, 2008.
2   Interview transcript from ABC Television's *Australian Story* program called 'Happy as Garry', between Caroline Jones and Garry McDonald, 11 November 2002.

CHAPTER 6

1   Access Economics, *Bipolar Disorder: Costs—An analysis for the burden of bipolar disorder and related suicide in Australia*, 2003, www.accesseconomics. com.au [26 March 2009].

CHAPTER 7

1   G. Parker and V. Manicavasagar, *Modelling and Managing the Depressive Disorders: A clinical guide*, Cambridge University Press, New York, 2005.
2   G. Parker (ed.), *Bipolar II Disorder: Modelling, measuring and managing*, Cambridge University Press, New York, 2008.
3   ibid.
4   M. Johnstone and A. Johnstone, *Living with a Black Dog: How to take care of someone with depression while looking after yourself*, Pan Macmillan, Sydney, 2008.

CHAPTER 8

1   Entrant 579 in Wigney, Eyers and Parker, *Journeys with the Black Dog*, p. 128.
2   K. Jamison, *Night Falls Fast: Understanding suicide*, Picador, London, 2000, p. 94.
3   J.L. Borges, 'A new refutation of time' in *Labyrinths*, Penguin Modern Classics, Harmondsworth, 1964, p. 269.

APPENDIX I

1   M. Teicher et al., 'Emergence of intense suicidal preoccupation during fluoxetine treatment', *American Journal of Psychiatry*, vol. 147, 1990, pp. 207–10.

2   G. Parker, 'Antidepressants on trial: how valid is the evidence?', *British Journal of Psychiatry*, vol. 194, 2009, pp. 1–3.

3   E.J. Garland, 'Facing the evidence: antidepressant treatment in children and adolescents', *Canadian Medical Association Journal*, vol. 170, 2004, pp. 489–91.

4   J. March et al., 'Fluoxetine, cognitive-behavioural therapy and their combination for adolescents with depression. Treatment for Adolescents with Depression Study (TADS) randomised control trial', *Journal of the American Medical Association*, 2004, vol. 292, pp. 807–20.

5   B. Vitiello, 'The Cutting Edge. Treatment of adolescent depression: what we have come to know', *Depression and Anxiety*, vol. 26, 2009, pp. 393–95.

APPENDIX II

1   Entrant 91 in Wigney, Eyers and Parker, *Journeys with the Black Dog*, p. 92.

2   Entrant 290 in Wigney, Eyers and Parker, *Journeys with the Black Dog*, p. 59.

Index